DAVID HENKEL

AGAINST THE UNITARIANS

A
TREATISE
ON
THE PERSON AND INCARNATION OF
JESUS CHRIST,
IN WHICH SOME OF THE PRINCIPAL
ARGUMENTS OF THE
UNITARIANS ARE
EXAMINED.

ORIGINALLY PUBLISHED IN 1830
BY ORDER OF THE EVANGELICAL
LUTHERAN TENNESSEE SYNOD.

WITH AN INTRODUCTION BY
DR. LOUIS A. SMITH

REPRISTINATION PRESS
MALONE, TEXAS

Introduction © 2002 by Dr. Louis A. Smith.
Used by Permission.

First Edition: 2002
Second Printing: 2011

Repristination Press
716 HCR 3424 E
Malone, TX 76660

ISBN 1-891469-36-3

Table of Contents

Defensor Fidei—The Polemical Theology of David Henkel
by Dr. Louis A. Smith 5
Against the Unitarians 65
Section I. One of the principal arguments of the Unitarians is,
that there can be no difference shewn between three divine persons
and three beings. This is examined, and the distinction between
the Father and the Son is somewhat elucidated. 67
Section II. Unitarians suppose that the Father is God alone
to the exclusion of Christ, because the terms God and Father
are synonymous, etc. This is examined, and it is more
particularly shewn that the Father and Christ are one being. 73
Section III. Christ is the only begotten Son of God.
It is shewn that although some attempt to prove because
he is a son, his Father is anterior to him; nevertheless
his sonship proves his eternal Deity. 83
Section IV. Some of the principal objections of the Unitarians
are examined. 92
Section V. Some arguments proving that Christ is God. 129
Section VI. The incarnation of the Son of God. 147

Defensor Fidei[1]
The Polemical Theology of David Henkel

In the year of our Lord, 1831, June 15 at 9:00A.M., near Lincolnton in Lincoln County, North Carolina, at the age of 36 years, one month and eleven days, David Henkel died. His last recorded words, spoken just before his death, were, "Oh Lord Jesus, Thou Son of God, receive my spirit."[2] With those words, David Henkel embraced, in his dying, the faith that he had preached and sought to defend during a ministerial career that spanned some 18 years—brief enough by common standard, yet long, given the young age at which he died.

David had been the Pastor of the Lutheran congregations in Lincoln County, North Carolina, which belonged to the Evangelical Lutheran Tennessee Synod since 1820 and to the North Carolina Synod prior to that year.[3] His career and the early years of the Tennessee Synod virtually coincide. Indeed, it was the family of David Henkel that was responsible for the founding of that synod, which was to play no small role in providing Lutherans in North America with the opportunity to remain Lutheran in substance as well as label, if for no other reason than that it was the impetus and talent of that synod, through the Henkel Press, its unofficial publishing instrument, that first gave Luther, Melanchthon, the other confessors at Augsburg and the formulators of Concord an English voice in the 1851 edition of the Book of Concord, the first complete English translation of the Lutheran Confessions.

I

The first battle front on which David undertook to defend the Lutheran confession of the biblical faith of the Church catholic involved holding the faith against those who were nominally "Lutheran" but thoroughly influenced by Reformed and pietistic versions of the faith.

David himself was both the cause and the *cause celebre* of the synod's coming into existence as a thoroughly confessional Lutheran Synod. For it was David, a younger member of this largely ministerial family, who seems to have first discovered the Lutheran confession and "converted" other family members to that position, which was to become the "Tennessee" position. And it was David's ordination to the Gospel ministry that occasioned the establishment of the synod itself in 1820.

David Henkel was born in Staunton, Virginia on May 4, 1795, the second youngest of six sons born to Paul and Elizabeth Henkel. Paul himself was a Lutheran Pastor, at that time operating under the auspices of the Pennsylania Ministerium as a traveling missionary to German speaking people in the Shenandoah Valley of Virginia and in North Carolina.[4] In 1800, Paul moved his family to Rowan County, North Carolina, a return to the place of his birth, in order to help Lutheran congregations there to deal with the onslaughts of the "revival" that was sweeping the area and he was instrumental in the founding of the North Carolina Synod in 1803.[5] This would not be the last synod whose founding would involve the Henkel family name.[6]

By the time David was 11 years old, the Henkel family had removed to New Market, Virginia, in the Shenandoah Valley, and, in addition to pastoral ministry by Paul and two older brothers of David, had embarked on a venture that would end up having great significance for American Lutheranism: The Henkel Press. In order to provide printed materials for German speaking people in western Virginia and the Carolinas as well as catechetical materials for use in their congregations, Ambrose Henkel, an elder brother to David, *walked* from New Market, Virginia to Hagerstown, Maryland in 1802–03 to learn the printing trade. He returned to set up shop in New Market in 1806 where the press remained in operation until 1971. Ambrose himself headed the printing company at first, but well before 1823, when he took up the ministerial office, his brother Solomon (who was also a physician) had already begun to play the dominant part in the administration of the press. In his early teens, David was apprenticed to Ambrose as a "printers devil."

By the time he reached his seventeenth birthday, David was on the road selling Henkel materials and taking subscriptions for future publications and reaching as far as South Carolina. While in South Carolina, he may have briefly studied theology with Pr. Godfrey (or Gottfried) Dreher, but by and large, apart from a brief period of elementary education under the tutelage of Simeon Yager in the New Market/Woodstock area of Virginia,[7] David seems to have been autodidact. Before his 17th birthday, he had, without any books to serve as model, authored an English/German grammar, which was considered to be a product of some merit.[8] At the age of 17, while in South Carolina, David entered the Gospel ministry as a "catechist," being licensed by a trio of pastors: Dreher, Johann Ludwig Markert and Jacob Sherer.[9]

The sparcity of synods, as well as their vast geographies, coupled with poor means of transportation, meant that at that time the ordination of pastors and the licensing of other ministries was a less than carefully regulated procedure, more than likely being carried out by one or more pastors. Furthermore, the fact that there were still no Lutheran seminaries meant that the training of pastors usually took on something of the form of an apprenticeship. Students for the ministry studied languages—Latin, Greek, Hebrew—and theology with an already ordained and practicing clergyman.

By the close of the Revolutionary War, three forces had come together to provide what semblance of ministerial order there was: the development of synods in Pennsylvania and New York as bodies that could authorize ministries; the demand for ministers and their services; and the vast geographical spread of congregations. The result, more a practical adjustment than a carefully devised plan, was something as follows.

On the basis of a first course of instruction, a person could be licensed as a "catechist." The licensing was an annual procedure, could be granted by two ordained pastors, and allowed the catechist (or "catechet," as it was regularly spelled at the time) to provide instruction, to read sermons, to conduct funerals and (where there was no pastor) to baptize in the congregation(s) to which they were assigned. An ordained minister was to come as often as possible to administer the Sacrament of the Altar. The catechist was presumed to be continuing his studies in Latin, Greek, and theology. After passing a first, or "fair," exam, the person could then be licensed as a "candidate," another annual procedure that allowed the person to exercise all of the *Acta Ministeriales* within the designated geography of the congregation that he served.[10] Further study and the passing of a second, or "good," exam would then see him ordained as pastor. The ordination could be carried out by two ordained pastors, without any further consultation. It may well be that it was Paul Henkel who brought this system to North Carolina and its adjacent States, since it was really he who was the initial connection between the North Carolina Synod and the Pennsylvania Ministerium, which seems to have been the place of its development.[11]

With hindsight, it is not hard to see the problems that such a system might induce. If the "candidate" can perform all the ministerial duties, even if it is in a limited area, just what does ordination confer? Or seen from the other way around, if ordination really does something, just what is to be made of the activities of those who are not yet ordained? They look to all the world like the acts of ministry, but are they?

As noted above, in 1812, at the ripe old age of 17, David was licensed as a catechist for work in South Carolina. In the fall of that same year, David, having moved to Lincoln County, North Carolina, was once again licensed as a catechist for that locale and succeeded his older brother, Philip, as Lutheran minister in those parts.[12] In October of the following year (1813), David appeared at the North Carolina Synod for the first time. This time, on petition of congregations in Lincoln County North Carolina, David's license was renewed. But at the same time some discomfort about his young age was expressed and a resolution was passed by synod that it would no longer be allowed for two ministers to authorize the licentiates. Instead, all licensings and ordinations would be carried out by the synod's authorization with a synodical examination.[13]

Later that year, in letter written from Lincoln County, North Carolina, David defended his youthful entrance into the ministry, to his own family, no less, on the basis of the call of the biblical prophets and apostles, who, on the basis of the testimony of Jeremiah, David considered to have been young men. The letter is addressed to his older brother, Solomon, but is intended for family consumption. At its conclusion, David indicates that he has received letters from his family telling him to come home and resume his work with the printing establishment. He is strong in his refusal to do so and suggests that the family should question their own motives in the request.[14]

The letter also contains a lengthy theological treatise in the course of which David maintains that it is rare to find genuine conversions or calls to the ministry late in life.[15] While no names are mentioned in the letter, it may be that this latter caveat is directed against one of the leading ministers of the North Carolina Synod, Gottlieb Shober (or Schober), who would become the leading antagonist to David, his family and the Tennessee Synod in the not too distant future. In 1810, Shober had been ordained at the age of 54.

A Moravian by background and inclination, Shober was something of a big-time operator in post-Revolutionary North Carolina. He was a lawyer who had also been a successful business man, Postmaster, Justice of the Peace and State Legislator. His secular activities seem to have put in him in some tension with the Moravian community in Salem, North Carolina. He was never ordained to the holy ministry by Moravians and seems to have had no theological training. He was, nonetheless, ordained by the Lutherans of the North Carolina Synod. At the synod during which he was ordained, he was also elected secretary of synod.[16] David's letter may be an early sign of the conflict that was to come.

The year 1814 produced another renewal of license for the now 19 year old David, but also a resolution not to license anyone under 21 years of age and then only after study with an ordained pastor. This latter element may well have been intended to detract from David's authority, since, as already noted, he was almost entirely self-educated.

In both 1813 and 1814, the synod was further agitated by the question of whether or not "candidates" could administer the Sacraments prior to their ordination. No action was taken on those occasions. At the synod of 1815, four senior pastors were absent, so no ordinations were held. Still, the question of whether laying on of hands, which was a part of the rite for ordaining pastors, should be done with all servants of the Word (i.e., catechists and candidates as well as pastors) was taken up. A final decision, however, was deferred until the following year. The now 20 year old David Henkel was licensed as a candidate.[17]

The following year (1816), the synod resolved to follow the Pennsylvania Ministerium rule with respect to licensing and ordination, thus creating four grades of ministers:

    1. Catechists—pursuing study and at the same time preaching, baptizing and catechizing, under synod supervision and care of one ordained minister.

    2. Candidates—still studying but performing all *Acta Min-*

isteriales in a specific congregation.

3. Ordained Deacons—who operate much as Candidates, but are considered ordained.

4. Pastors—who have completed 3 years of systematic study under an ordained minister and have studied languages "somewhat."

Based on the deliberations of the prior year (1815), a compromise of sorts was worked out whereby the licentiates (both catechists and candidates) would receive their licenses in public ceremony, including the laying on of hands.

Evidence of the difficulties experienced within the North Carolina Synod over the issue of ordination and the laying of hands can be seen in a pair of letters written by Robert Johnson Miller to Shober in the months surrounding the Synod of 1816. In July of 1816, Miller expresses his satisfaction at having heard that the Pennsylvania Ministerium has taken "the scriptural measure" of introducing a "secondary order" for younger ministers. In the following December, Miller, who was not at the 1816 synod, expresses his dismay at some of the "scenes" that took place. He also indicates that he has had some trouble with David Henkel and at least one leader in his congregations. Taking Miller's report at face value, it seems that Miller was accused of saying that David and his colleague, Daniel Moser, had no proper ministerial authority and were therefore impostors. Miller maintains that he has never disputed that they had received authority from the synod and that in one case he had acknowledged David's authority to administer the Lord's Supper. What he did question, however, was whether the synod had received from Christ the power to license in the way that it did. Since ordination and the Supper are not ceremonies or rites but "divine institutions," the Church is not at liberty to depart from them.

In the earlier letter, Miller also gave witness to problems that have developed between some of the synod and the Henkel family. He refers to a "cloud appearing on the Northeast horizon" of the synod. It is clear that the Henkels are intended, but Miller points, not to the person of David, but of Paul, whom he calls a "would be Pope." While the precise nature of the antagonism is not specified, it seems to revolve around the Henkel desire to remain more definitively Lutheran. The indication is that the Henkels have pointed toward a possible split in the North Carolina Synod over that matter and that Paul has suggested that such a split would also mean a rupture between North Carolina and the Pennsylvania Ministerium. Johnson himself believes that the Henkels may well leave, but doubts that the relationship to Pennsylvania will go with them. In this respect, Johnson was prophetic.[18]

That the target of Johnson's words should be the Henkel family as a whole probably points to a growing theological influence on David's part with respect to his entire family. Prior to this time, David's family had not shown any particular conviction about things Lutheran. An earlier catechism produced by Paul shows more than a little Reformed influence in spite of its use of Luther's Small Catechism.[19] And as early as 1812 and as late as 1818 David's oldest brother, Solomon, was involved in conversations that, if completed, would have put Lutherans into union with the Reformed and Episcopal Church, respectively.[20]

At the 1816 synod, the secretary of the synod, Gottlieb Shober, was directed to compile "all the rules adopted by this Synod and to publish them in the English language."[21] This resolution would end up having a major significance in the split between North Carolina and Tennessee.

Having now reached his majority (21 years of age), David had hopes of being ordained. The congregations that he served also entertained the hope and gave it concrete expression by way of a series of petitions addressed to the synod requesting David's ordination.[22] But in the midst of the on-going turmoil over licensing and ordination in general, no ordination was carried out. It was, however, recommended at this synod that David Henkel be given full power to administer the sacraments "in all our churches." But not be ordained.[23] David himself, for this date (Oct. 22, 1816), records in his diary that "with great dissatisfaction ... at 4:00 p.m. I was ordained by Geo. Shober." Just who was dissatisfied is not stated, but it probably refers to the protest of Pr. C. A. Storch, the synod president for that year, over the use of laying on of hands for licentiates.

What is important to note, however, is that David records this as being "ordained" and while the synod minutes do not record it as such, nevertheless, the privilege of administering the Sacraments "in all our churches," was explicitly granted; a privilege that went beyond the usual licentiate.[24]

That extension of privilege seems to carry some importance in view of a conflict that would arise the following Spring between David and Shober, who was not merely the secretary of synod, but a truly a dominant force in its activities.

It seems that at Christmas time, 1816, David had preached in several congregations that had been left vacant by Pr. John Ludwig Markert. These would be the congregations in Davidson and Davie Counties that Markert had vacated earlier in 1816 to return to his native Ohio, as well as Indiana and Illinois, as a missionary pastor.[25] Shober took offense at David's presence, complaining that these congregations, at the October 1816 synod, had been committed into his care and that David's preaching there, without giving Shober notice, was a "rambling abroad on Christmas" and "a breach of the rules of polite education" and an "offense against a senior minister." David, in response, protests that had Shober taken the time to ask, he could have determined that in delivering the sermons he, David, was merely honoring a commitment that he had made prior to the preceding synod, when he could not have known that they would be assigned to Shober and so was in no position to give him notice.[26] As further evidence of his integrity in the matter he points out to Shober that some of the people in those congregations had solicited him to become their pastor and that he had refused; that some asked him to confirm their children, which he likewise refused to do, unless they could get no one else to do it.[27]

It is highly unlikely that this is the first point of conflict between the Shober and David Henkel. In fact, shortly before this event a genuine conflict with regard to the faith itself had made its way into the public arena. In 1814 Shober, promising, "to dish up some new well seasoned and agreeable sauce, or views in religious conceptions, in order to induce immortal souls to reflect on the *manner* of their future existence, and in good earnest to prepare to meet their Lord and Redeemer with fruits of faith and love ...,"[28] began to translate from German the speculations of Johann Heinrich Jung (a.k.a. Heinrich Stilling) or, as he was regularly referred to, "Jung-Stilling." Jung-Stilling (1740–1817) had been educated by his father in radical Pietism and later came under the influence of the lower Rhenish Pietism known as "*Die Stillen im Lande*," from which his popular name was derived. In 1762, he underwent a conversion experience, but by

1770 he had come under the influence of the Enlightenment. A varied career had seen him be a tailor and a schoolmaster. He had studied medicine and practiced as an ophthalmologist and from 1781 to 1803 had taught economics in Marburg. A friend of Goethe and Herder, he had been a member of the Reformed Church in Germany but late in life had become acquainted with the Moravians[29] and it may well be that it is by that route that Shober became acquainted with his writing. In 1815, vol.1 of *Scenes in The World of the Spirit*, Shober's translation of Jung-Stilling, appeared, published by The Henkel Press(!) in New Market. It was not long thereafter that David Henkel published a sermon that moved in a quite opposite direction.

The Essence of The Christian Religion: A Sermon by David Henkel, was preached to the congregation at White Haven, Lincoln County, N.C. on Sunday, September 8, 1816 at the celebration of the Lord's Supper. The congregation itself is said to have requested the publication.[30]

David begins the sermon by noting the controversies that the Christian religion has stirred among those who have tried to interpret it, and moves to bypass the controversies by appeal to what he considers a universal anthropological truth, viz. all reasonable beings strive for happiness. His further analysis maintains that the "Love is the fountain felicity," and that in creating human beings after his own image, God has communicated to them a portion of love. This leads him to the Augustinian consideration that the misery in which humanity actually finds itself is the result of a mis-oriented love. Human beings love, but they do not love the "the proper object of love, which is God."[31]

From this point of departure, David argues for the ignorance of humankind with respect to God as the cause of human misery and that the restoration to happiness comes about through the proper knowledge of God through Jesus and reception of His atonement *by the means of grace*.[32] This emphasis on the means of grace is a mark of David's thought throughout his career, and is at the root of many of his conflicts both within the Lutheran community and with other religious denominations.

While I know of no recorded reaction of Shober to this sermon, its anti-Pietistic bent and emphasis on the means of grace may well have come as something of a shock to him. For it seems that in the preceding year, he had counted on David's support in selling the book. In March of that year (1815), Shober had written to David requesting him to obtain subscribers for his forth-coming translation of Jung-Stilling. And while he understands that David hasn't yet read the book, he also assumes that what knowledge of Jung-Stilling David does have will lead him to be supportive. "You have no doubt entertained a good opinion of Stilling's writing ...," wrote Shober.[33] He was clearly mistaken.

A year after the preaching of *The Essence of Christianity*, another tract from David again seems to have the speculative Pietism promoted by Shober as its target. *The Loud Trumpet of Futurity* appears to set a thorough going biblical eschatology in the place of Jung-Stillung's pietistic and moralistic speculations.[34] A letter from the above mentioned Miller to Shober, dated July 15, 1817, indicates that this tract too was originally a sermon; of four hours duration, no less![35]

In 1817, David's ordination was again put off, but it seems that it was designated to take place at the next synod. Since it was also decided to change the regular time of the synod from the late October date that it had up occupied until that time to Trinity Sunday, no meeting was scheduled for 1818, but instead, synod adjourned until Trinity Sunday 1819.[36]

Before the 19 months had elapsed, however, several things had taken place, both with respect to David Henkel and with respect to the synod as a whole, which conspired both to delay David's ordination yet again and finally to rupture the North Carolina Synod. With respect to the North Carolina Synod itself, the critical event of the 19 month interlude between synods was the stirring that would finally lead to the founding of the General Synod in 1820. Early in 1819, the officers of the North Carolina Synod received a communication from the Pennsylvania Synod. The letter invited North Carolina to send a representative to the 1819 Pennsylvania Synod which was to meet in Baltimore on Trinity Sunday, the date that had been fixed for the North Carolina Synod to meet. The purpose of meeting with the Pennsylvanians was to explore a more general church union. This was a meeting that was right up Shober's alley. The then-secretary of the North Carolina Synod was not infrequent in issuing statements which expressed sentiments leaning toward ignoring doctrinal differences among the various Christian bodies.[37] His great desire to participate in the Pennsylvania meeting led to the re-dating of the 1819 North Carolina Synod to a date some six weeks earlier. The redating was at the impetus of Shober, with the cooperation of Pr. Storch, the president. It was confirmed after the fact by the April Synod through a resolution that allowed for a special synod to meet urgent circumstances with the specification that its transactions would be in effect until the next regular synod.[38]

At this early meeting, called "the untimely meeting" in the Henkel tradition, there was just a partial attendance. Four pastors and six licentiates were absent with the complaint that the short notice of the change had not allowed them sufficient time to arrange attendance. Socrates Henkel maintains that some of the ministers did not receive notification of the change in meeting time until after the meeting had actually taken place and this is borne out by a letter sent to the North Carolina Synod by Philip Henkel, at the time residing in eastern Tennessee, as well as a letter from David Henkel to his brother Solomon dated August 9, 1819.[39]

David himself, however, was present at the "untimely meeting." By the time of his arrival at the meeting, the expectation of ordination, which had seemed to be so firm in October of 1817, may have been reduced to little more than an ephemeral hope. Even before the synod there had been indication that David would have to listen to a variety of charges that would be laid against him. Three weeks prior to the synod, David was trying to gather evidence in his defense.[40] The charges would finally be three-fold. First, there were charges of disturbing the peace of the Church and the civil community which arose from conflict with some Presbyterian ministers in Lincoln Co. who resented his "excessive championing" of Lutheran teaching. Second, there were some charges that were doctrinal in nature. David was accused of teaching "transubstantiation," that Baptism was regeneration, and that he had the personal power to forgive sins. Finally, a Mr. Andrew Hoyle charged David with "rash behavior" aimed at destroying Mr. Hoyle's reputation. Mr. Hoyle would turn out to be the formal bearer of all of the charges at the synod. It is clear from the record that some, if not all, of the charges had been hinted at well prior to the April Synod, since David, in the preceding weeks, had begun to secure evidence that would exonerate him. Hoyle, a participant in the life of David's Lincoln County congregations despite being a "German Presbyterian" (Hoyle's own self designation), was actually present at a meeting at Philadelphia Church, one of David's congregations, when David was preparing his defense. At that time, Mr. Hoyle told David in the presence of witnesses that he was not intending to bring charges against David; and therefore it was not necessary to prepare himself; and that had he (Hoyle) intended to bring the charges he would have notified David of the same.[41] Yet, three weeks later, Hoyle stood before the North Carolina Synod as David's accuser! What had happened in the meantime? While matters are not completely clear, the following emerges from contemporary testimony. First, Hoyle was in contact with a fellow antagonist of David's, Adam Casner. Casner's involvement with David will be enlarged on below. Suffice it for the moment to record that on March 20, 1819, Casner had been excommunicated by the Philadelphia congregation.[42] There is testimony that in the weeks preceding the Easter Monday Synod, Hoyle sent Casner to the home of Synod President Storch to ask whether he (Hoyle) should bring certificates or depositions against David to the Synod. Just who initiated this contact we do not know. Storch's instruction was to bring depositions. At the same time, Casner filed a complaint about David, undoubtedly concerning the excommunication.[43] All in all, there appears to be some influence on the part of the synod leadership in changing Hoyle's mind about appearing at the synod against David.

The antagonism of Mr. Hoyle, largely personal in nature, appears to be based on two events. Mr. Hoyle claims in his letter of accusation that he was a "German Presbyterian" (undoubtedly meaning Reformed) but that for a number of years, since there were no Reformed pastors in the area, he associated with the Lutheran congregation and, although never formally joining, went so far in his support as to pay the stipend of the Lutheran pastor, and that he was treated as being in full communion by Phillip Henkel while he was the Lutheran minister in Lincoln County. This arrangement seemed to work all right, Hoyle maintains, until David became the minister, at about the same time that some English Presbyterians entered the scene. Then, not Hoyle, but a number of others began to associate with the Presbyterians, which, so Hoyle claims, made David envious. As a result, David is alleged to have made harsh statements against Reformed Christians, including the claim that since they do not believe in the real corporeal presence of Christ in the Lord's Supper, they are idolaters.

Mr. Hoyle also brought with him a letter from a Methodist preacher, James Hall, who had heard David preach at a service of holy communion charged David with having taught transubstantiation, that Baptism was regeneration, that believers were perfect, and that the laying on of hands was necessary in confirmation. While David's deputies at the synod denied the assertions, the senior ministers of the synod opted to believe Hall and the synod secretary, Gottlieb Shober, claimed to have a letter from David which would substantiate the charge. When David asked for the letter to be read, Shober refused.[44]

The letter in question was most likely a letter that David had written to Shober in October of 1818. It was, practically speaking, a piece of exegesis of I Corinthians. It may well be that as a part of David's study as a "candidate," Shober was to be his "supervisor." In this letter, David has argued for the omnipresence of the humanity of Christ. Shober responds that while seven-eighths of the hearers may well be amazed at the erudition of the argument and the other one-eighth will shake their heads at the notion of something which is to be believed but is not explainable, "to none will it effect conviction of the necessity of spiritual regeneration and of adopting him as their God & Saviour."[45]

It is clear, however, that Shober's Pietism moved him to deny a Word constituted and consecration based objective presence of the Body and Blood of Christ in the Sacrament. In his letter in response to David, he refers to a prior conversation between the two on the matter at hand and says, "...when Mr. Henkel consecrates Bread and Wine, it is the body and blood of our Saviour, *to such with whom he can unite, but to those who are not of pure heart & yet partake, and that with reverence, the Spirituality of the true essence does not unite with their souls, they eat and drink bread and wine, for they have not such faith, love and humility as enables them to be possessed of the divine essence.*"[46]

As far as Shober is concerned, there is yet a third group of participants, those who partake without reverence. These truly impious participants eat and drink judgment on themselves "for eating and drinking the consecrated elements — but not for partaking the body and blood of Jesus for they have not partaken thereof."[47]

The letter also indicates that Shober is disturbed by David's practice of pastoral absolution. And he claims that "creditable people from both Lutheran and Reformed Churches have reported that David has taught that "Whosoever is baptized & partakes of the Supper wants no further repentance but that also whosoever teaches other doctrine, he is a false teacher." Shober maintains that David's position gives people a false security and makes it easy "for an adulterous heart to be absolved by Mr. Henkel, and as a seal to receive from Mr. Henkel the sacrament, who by his fine words made bread body & wine blood..."[48]

Apparently David heard of these reports before this occasion and requested that Shober name his sources. But Shober offered only an examination at the synod; presumably the doctrinal portion of the "trial" in 1819.[49]

The charge that David had sought to destroy Hoyle's reputation resulted from an oath that David had taken before Mr. Hoyle as a Justice of the Peace. A lawsuit had arisen between a certain Mrs. Susannah Williams and a Mr. David Lineberger. David, acting as pastor, tried to affect a compromise and even offered to pay some of the costs in order to bring about a peace. The lawsuit went on, however, and David was called as a witness. In a deposition made before Mr. Hoyle, he swore that he had not told anyone that he knew of an arrangement between the litigants. Later, however, he recalled that he had said something to that effect to one person and went to Hoyle to inform him of the fact. Hoyle proceeded to tell either Mrs. Williams or a friend of hers, the above mentioned Adam Casner, and word was spread that David had committed perjury. In the ensuing defense and counter defense, charges were hurled back and forth, David claiming that Hoyle had slandered him and threatening a lawsuit, while Hoyle claimed that David's "rash behavior" had damaged his reputation.[50] It is also this case that led to the excommunication of Casner mentioned above.

Finally, in, with and under the charges made at the synod, there appears to be a matter of ongoing doctrinal conflict with at least one leading minister of the synod. Socrates Henkel, in his *History of the Evangelical Lutheran Tennessee Synod*, reports that sometime in the vicinity of the 1817 Synod an unidentified "leading minister" accused David Henkel of teaching contrary to the doctrinal position of the

Church. (He does not date the event, but mentions it in this general time frame.) David defended himself by appeal to his Latin Book of Concord. His opponent questioned the accuracy of David's translation and this left the matter unresolved. Not too long thereafter, David came into possession of a German Book of Concord, which now sustained his case in the common language of the congregations. Socrates Henkel does not name the minister.[51] David Jay Webber, in a recent article "Confessing the Faith in the Language of America," has speculated that "the leading minister" was none other than the above multi-mentioned Gottlieb Shober.[52] This is possible, given Shober's continuing Moravian connections, his latitudinarian doctrinal views, and his age advantage (He was 54 at the time of his ordination in 1810) over this "young whippersnapper." But the general time frame and other personalities mentioned in the story make Pr. Carl Storch an equally likely candidate. And there is evidence that Storch and David entered in direct doctrinal conflict at the 1819 Synod.

The matters of doctrine that were in conflict at this synod were in fact a symptom of a growing split between David and those who were beginning to follow his confessional Lutheran lead and the senior ministers in the orientation toward churchly and doctrinal affairs. An illustration of the division can be seen in an episode that is to be dated around the turn of the year from 1817 to 1818. At this time, David and his congregation in the Beaver Dam and Long Creek areas of Lincoln County were trying to erect a church meeting house that would be exclusively Lutheran as opposed to the common "union church" structures of the day. Without using the term "Lutheran," their proposal to Commissioner William Vickers outlined confessional Lutheran doctrinal positions as tests to be applied to the preachers seeking to use the building. First among those principles was "that Jesus Christ is real God and man and that his manhood is taken up into the Godhead and that therefore he, according to his human nature, is almighty and all knowing and everywhere present together with possessing every other divine attribute."[53]

Not only did Vickers refuse to accept the conditions, this specific item seems to have been put forward in the charges against David at the synod in 1819. David, of course, turned the whole thing around in his *Carolinian Herald of Liberty* where he charges the synodical leadership, and specifically the president, Storch, with deviance from Lutheran doctrine and the biblical evidence for it.[54] This particular statement concerning the "manhood" of Christ was read at the 1819 synod, and President Storch said in response that such could not be true. David responded that such was the doctrine of the Bible, to which Storch said "if 500 Bibles say so, I do not believe it."[55]

But whether the person in Socrates Henkel's story is Shober or Storch, it is not difficult to guess the issues that were involved. In one way or another they would all have to do with issues of Christology and the means of grace.

At this 1819 synod, the matters pertaining to doctrine were dismissed. The personal charges against David were upheld, however, and the synod, much to the chagrin of David's Philadelphia congregation, overturned Casner's excommunication. At the end of the day, Hoyle and David shook hands and were (apparently) reconciled, but Hoyle publicly announced victory and vindication.[56] More serious yet, the synod leadership took disciplinary action against David. Not only was he not ordained, his license was reduced from candidate to catechist, with the note that if David could be shown to have mended his ways over the next six months, he would be restored to candidate status.

But six weeks is a much shorter time than six months, and six weeks later, while Shober (having gotten himself elected delegate) was attending the Baltimore meeting, Philip Henkel, several ministers from Tennessee, several lay delegates and the candidates, David Henkel and Joseph Bell, showed up at the place and time that had been set at the 1817 adjournment. They contacted the aging and ill Storch, president of synod at the time, who lived nearby and asked him to come to the church to open the synod. Storch refused, claiming both illness and that the synod had already been held. He finally allowed the Church to be opened for worship, although he prohibited any synod business to be conducted there. This prohibition was respected by the group that had gathered, so after the worship, those present left the church building and conducted their business outside under some nearby shade trees. Included among the business was the ordaining of both David Henkel and Joseph Bell to the full ministry of Word and Sacrament, in accord, it was maintained, with the 1817 resolution of synod.

Two years later, David would defend the legality of his ordination by pointing to the license that he had been issued in April of

1819, on the occasion of his degrading. The license, signed by Storch and Shober as the officers of the synod, specified that its validity was to last "until the next conference."⁵⁷ While it can hardly be doubted that Storch and Shober were thinking of an 1820 Synod, David's quick mind put the words of the license together with the words of the resolution about special synods and saw the constitutionally set meeting of Trinity Sunday 1819 as an opportunity to undo the deeds of the "untimely Synod." With David's ordination, nothing less than the personal authority of the "Alte Herren"—Storch, Shober and Miller—had been challenged. Obviously things were in place for a rupture, and the following year it happened.

Clearly, David was not the kind of person to take his wrist being slapped without response. In the months following his ordination, he set about gathering certificates that would support his case with respect to Hoyle's charges and those of disturbing the peace. But it was not only against the synod leadership that David had to defend himself. Even his father, Paul, and his brother, Solomon, had to be convinced of David's cause.

There is plenty of evidence that David was less than a favorite son of his father and that Solomon stood at his father's side in this regard. We have already had the occasion to mention David's defense of his early entry into the ministry to his family. Shober was able to produce letters from both Paul and Solomon which reflect negatively on David. In January of 1818, Paul called David "hot-headed" and indicates that communication between father and son had broken down. On May 26 of 1819, i.e. between the April synod and that of Trinity Sunday, Paul writes to Shober, "The information respecting David and his conduct, if it is true, is disagreeable; but the remedy applied to him may be good. It is a pity that he misuses his talents; but I could never bring him to think and act otherwise."⁵⁸ And in the same time frame, Solomon wrote to Shober saying, "It is most miserable that David cannot come to right again. ... That you have reduced him in office is right if it only brings him to more humility; but I fear his pride will not admit of it. . . ."⁵⁹

However, perhaps the depth of antagonism is best shown by a pair of letters from David to Solomon, one shortly before the 1819 Trinity Sunday synod and one shortly after. In the first letter, David actually threatens Solomon with a lawsuit, if, after receiving this notice, he nevertheless prints the minutes of the April synod, which David derisively refers to as the "Bastard Synod."

The second letter, written after the Trinity synod, spells out the constitutional reasons for the illegitimacy of the April synod, on the one hand, and legitimacy of the Trinity meeting, on the other. It also contains a plea for Solomon to sever his connections with the North Carolina leaders to whom David refers as "Covenant Breakers." Clearly, Solomon had not yet come to espouse David's cause.[60]

As we have seen, following his demotion to catechist and his subsequent ordination, David set about refuting the charges that had been laid against him. Since the charges were made public in local newspapers, David would, in the end, make his defense an equally public matter. In this undertaking, David seems to have had the full support and cooperation, as well as the participation, of the congregations that he served. Congregational committees reported that they conducted a careful investigation and concluded that the charges were not valid. David published the reports of these committees in his *Carolinian Herald of Liberty*.[61]

These reports also indicate that David's father, the much respected Paul, was concerned enough for his son to conduct some inquiries of his own into David's circumstance. No doubt, at least some of this investigation was a matter of meeting with the local committees. As a result of these inquiries, Paul became convinced that David had been mistreated by the North Carolina Synod officials. Coming to accept his son's vindication seems to have earned the father some public censure, undoubtedly from the synod officials among others. Nevertheless, the result seems to have been that the Henkel family was solidly behind David and his Lutheran cause.[62]

While David's conflict with the old leadership of the North Carolina Synod was already on the record in a variety of ways, the Carolinian Herald of Liberty is the first published direct attack on the theological position of the leadership. Here he deals with their deviation from Lutheran doctrine on the basis of Scripture, the Augsburg Confession and Luther's Small Catechism. In dealing with their deviation from the teaching of the real bodily presence of Christ in the Sacrament of the Altar, David cites and critiques the synod leadership's own answer to James Hill and refutes it on the basis of their own translation of Article X of the Augustana. But David also notes that the translation which had been used in the synod constitution was weak. It is not as "emphatic" as it could be were the German text of CA X to be rendered literally.

In this same connection, David also maintained that Pr. Storch, at that time the president of the synod, had publicly denied that the humanity of Christ was taken up into the Godhead and that when shown that such was the Biblical teaching, Storch denied the authority of the Bible maintaining that he would not believe it "if 500 Bibles said so."[63]

But David did not merely critique his opponents. Rather, he used the occasion to set forth a positive doctrine of the Sacrament. In order to do so, he adopted the form of the Formula of Concord of 1577. David lays out the *status controversiae*; it is, "Whether the real body of Christ, which was crucified and His real blood are present... and are administered not only to believers but also to unbelievers. The opponents to Lutherans say no—but we say yes."[64] The issue of the Real Presence of Christ's Body and Blood in the Blessed Sacrament of the Altar, as David sees it, comes to clarification in what has been called the *manducatio impiorum*. This is, of course, classic Reformation argumentation.

Because the issue here becomes somewhat subtle, David goes on to refine the opponents in two classes. The first group, he says treat bread and wine as "'emblems, representations or memorials' and hold that the words of institution are not to be taken literally. The second group is willing to admit that *true believers* may eat and drink the Body and Blood of Christ spiritually, by 'ascending with their mind to heaven...'" David, however, holds to the obvious clarity of the *Verba Testamenti*, Christ's own words at the Supper.

This, in turn, becomes the occasion for a serious exegetical consideration of tropes and literal speech, emblems and realities. Since much of this discussion is repeated in David's *Heavenly Flood of Regeneration* and his *Answer to Mr. Joseph Moore, The Methodist*, treatment of it will be deferred until we discuss those works. But for the moment, the following merits mention. Since, in this writing, David is dealing with others who claim the Lutheran designation, he recites a host of traditional Lutheran arguments to defend the Lutheran doctrine of the Real Presence against both transubstantiation and 'symbolic' doctrines.

He charges, for example, both those who teach transubstantiation and those who teach symbolic doctrines of the Supper with idolatry because, he maintains, both offer substitutes for Christ. Transubstantiation, may intend otherwise, but since, for David, the transubstantiation doesn't actually happen, the result is none the less idolatrous. Teachers of symbolic doctrines consciously offer a substitute, the "emblem," for Christ, the reality.[65] The New Testament, as Christ's last will and testament, must convey realities and not symbols, says David, much to the point.

Further, David maintains, a ritual fraction of the bread is not a valid symbol of what happened to Christ in the Passion because, "not a bone of His body was broken." (John 19:36) Nor does the wine/blood flow from a piercing of the bread/body. Although no reference are provided to give us a glimpse of the source of David's argument, it is totally reminiscent of late sixteenth century Lutheran arguments aimed at Calvinists, who maintained the necessity of a ritual fraction for a valid Sacrament, treating the Sacrament of the Altar as if it were something of a divine audio-visual aid.[66]

David deals with memorial theories of the Sacrament by pointing out that the words which are cited to prove such teaching, "Do this in remembrance of Me," do not refer to a dead or absent person. Christ is alive and therefore to remember Him is to trust in His help. But such trust itself implies a living presence rather than an absence.[67]

Further, David stresses that the relationship between faith and the Sacrament move *from* the sacrament *to* faith and not the other way around. Faith must have a proper foundation, he maintains. Mere bread and wine could not be such. The presence of Christ, however, can be and is just such a proper foundation for faith. Therefore, David can say that the "Good" of the Sacrament creates faith; faith does not create the "Good" of the Sacrament. And contrariwise, unbelief cannot undo the words of the Lord.[68]

What is, perhaps, unique to the discussion of the Sacrament in the *Carolinian Herald*, is David's exegetical discussion of 1 Corinthians 11:29, "For he that eateth and drinketh unworthily, eateth and drinketh damnation to himself, not discerning the Lord's body." This text, obviously a key locus for the doctrine of the *manducatio impiorum*, receives the following treatment from David in an extended note. First, David acknowledges that this text has terrified many people and kept them away from the Supper out of fear that they were not properly converted. Thus David begins his exegesis of this important text in a pastoral context. His goal will be to counter this pietistic inward turn and to encourage reception of the Sacrament.

David's first move is to examine the Corinthian/biblical context in which the text appears. It does not, he maintains, deal with the unconverted, but with Corinthians who are already Christians. On the basis of 1 Corinthians 11:20-22, David sees that the Church in Corinth was accustomed to celebrating the Eucharist in the context of a feast. At the feast, some over-indulged, becoming drunk and unruly. Thus, the apostle refers to their drunk and unruly behavior as eating and drinking "unworthily." And David immediately emphasizes that word "unworthily" is an adverb, which describes the behavior, rather than an adjective describing the persons.

David then goes on to examine the word translated as "damnation." The Greek word, David maintains, refers to a temporal judgment rather than to an eternal judgment. He finds this analysis to be confirmed by the apostle in 1 Corinthians 11:30-32, which interprets the judgment in terms of chastisement. And the chastisement is specified as being in order that they "might not be condemned with the world." The object of the chastisement was, therefore, the repentance of those who behaved in a drunk and unruly manner. It is, he offers, the correction of a "kind father" intended to drive those who fall under it to Christ, the merciful Savior who is always seeking the lost. Thus, for David, the text becomes a vivid example of the preaching of Law and Gospel within the Church. Such preaching will produce proper faith which will bring the penitent to the Supper and not fill them with scruples that would keep them away.[69]

When we remember that in this discussion David's opponents are people who call themselves "Lutheran," we can see in this David's effort to call the Lutheran Church back to its biblical and confessional moorings.

II

In 1822, David published an essay entitled *Heavenly Flood of Regeneration*. The title page indicates that the essay was published "by order and under the patronage of the Evangelical Lutheran Book Society of Lincoln County, North Carolina."[70] The book is intended as a positive statement of Lutheran teaching with respect to holy Baptism. Of course, this does not mean that the book is devoid of polemic. That could hardly be the case, given that the Lutheranism which David espoused was under constant attack not only from within the Lutheran fold, but also from other denominations, which not only were not Lutheran in the first place, but were religious groups where Pietism and Rationalism had made strong inroads.

The book is divided into seven chapters, or "sections" as they are called. Each section presents an "argument" and then a "confirmation" of the argument. The first section argues for what might be called a "sacramental" principle with respect to the workings of God. "God employs external means in the distribution of his blessings. Man cannot rationally expect to receive his blessings without the use of the proper means: Upon this ground the utility of holy baptism is inferred. etc."

Drawing analogies from nature and from Holy Scripture, David holds up what has been called God's "mediated immediacy"; i.e., while God Himself is the worker, He does His work through a variety of "media." Moreover, says David, these "media" are characteristically "simple." This simplicity, however, is well-suited to the task of actually glorifying God, the Worker. "The feebler the instrument seems by which mighty works are wrought, the plainer the omnipotent hand of God is to be seen."[71]

The section closes with a long citation from Luther's treatise, *Against the Heavenly Prophets*, which David cites according to the work of Dr. J.H.C. Helmuth.[72]

The second section presents the argument that Baptism is made up of two elements, the Word of the Gospel and the water. Therefore, Baptism is "a rich flood of grace." "The Word of the Gospel is Spirit and Life. This, with the water, constitutes Holy Baptism. hence it is a rich flood of grace, etc."[73]

The argument in this section is essentially the argument of Luther's catechisms: "baptism is not simple water only; but with it the word of God is connected.... Thus it may properly be called a visible or elementary word. Without the word, it would be no Christian baptism."[74] But, David argues, since the Word of God is the principle thing in Baptism, whatever is true of the word must also be true of Baptism. "[I]f the gospel-word possess a regenerating virtue, baptism possesses the same. ... If I deny baptism to be a means of regeneration, I must deny the word as being the same; for the word and water in baptism are not to be separated."[75]

At this point, David launches into an attack on those who reject the notion that Baptism is the means of regeneration and opt instead for the view that it is "no more than an emblem, or a representation." David couples this notion with contempt for the outward Word, which is seen by the holders or the "emblematic" or "representational" view as "a dead letter." Such as hold this view, says David, also maintain that it takes some "extraordinary operation" not necessarily connected to the Word for the sinner to be converted. When David analyses why this should be so, he comes to the conclusion that such folk cannot deal with the obvious fact that Baptism and the external Word of God frequently seem to fail in their purpose. "Now it can be easily accounted for why such teach baptism to be an emblem. ... [I]t would be contrary to the wisdom of God to give or offer his grace in vain; which would be the case, if he sincerely offered it to any whom he knew would finally perish."[76] All of which is to say that the separation of the Spirit and the Word which is the at the root of the denial of regeneration to Baptism, is no more than the human effort to save God the embarrassment of having His sovereignty compromised.

But David, at close to his polemical best, will not let the matter rest there. He will pursue the logic of the opposing argument to it's dreadful conclusion. "If God offers his gospel to us, but does not with it grant the power that we may receive it, we certainly would be excusable for not receiving it; and he would justly be accused as 'a hard man, reaping where he had not sown.'"[77]

In the third section, David turns his attention to baptismal *mandatum* in Matthew 28. It is here that the true dignity and value and majesty of holy Baptism are to be found, and this in a two-fold way. For the dignity, value and majesty of holy Baptism are derived both from the fact that it is commanded by the Savior and the fact that it is carried out in the name of the holy and blessed Trinity. "Every command," says David, "owes its importance to the dignity and authority of the person from whom it originates ... But whose command is baptism? It is neither of a beggar, nor of a temporal king—but of the King of kings and Lord of lords; of incarnate Jehovah. Hence its infinite importance."[78] He goes on to compare the authority conveyed in holy Baptism with the authority conveyed by a note of pardon signed by a governor. The effectiveness of the pardon depends entirely on the name that is signed on the document. And the pardon carried out is of benefit to the one named in the pardon. Since such is also the case with holy Baptism, the critical question is whose name is signed therein and for whose benefit it is given. The answer to these critical questions is that the name of "Jehovah" is signed and it is for the benefit of sinners that it is given.[79]

David further develops this argument with a discussion of the name of God in Holy Scripture and concludes: "God's name in Holy Scripture is frequently put for himself ... God's name, in this sense, is God. To call on and to worship his name is to call on and worship God."[80] Now, since the name of God is the same as God Himself and that name is in Baptism, David infers the following:

1. Baptism is no more a human invention than the name of God is and thus it must be a flood of grace since, like God's name, it saves and thus redounds to the glory of God.

2. Baptism is very holy because the name of God which is in it is three-fold and thus thrice holy. This holiness is joined to the water and with it constitutes our Baptism. "With what holy awe ought we to think of our baptism!"

3. God's name is the fundamental thing in Baptism. Therefore it cannot be denied that it is a saving means or "flood of regeneration." It is, therefore, lamentable when people make light of it.

4. Since God's name is in Baptism, faith is exercised in it. "Faith must have a foundation on which it must rest, which is God's holy name in baptism. ... Therefore it [faith] cannot be a virtue in us that is meritorious ... [I]f our faith is not created by the word and God's name, what else can it be but a self-work?"[81]

In order to confirm his position, David provides his own translation of a large portion of Luther's *Large Catechism*.[82] To my knowledge, this is the first English rendering of this piece of the Lutheran confessional heritage.

The fourth section of the book deals with the relationship between the Holy Spirit and Baptism under the theme of "Holy Baptism is the ordinary means of regeneration." David begins from the text in John 3:3, "Verily, verily I say unto thee, except a man be born again, he cannot see the kingdom of God." And he immediately adds the interpretative words of John 3:5: "...except a man be born of water and the spirit he cannot enter the kingdom of God."

David begins his consideration of the matter by noting a strange contradiction. Most Christian denominations, he says, confess that by this second birth a "new Spiritual child" is brought to life. But then they turn around and say that Baptism is not the ordinary means of regeneration. But they can accomplish this only by tinkering with the text, which in the case of the present text means that they take the position that the water mentioned in the text doesn't really mean water. "They know if the term water in this passage signifies that element which is generally so called, that it could not be otherwise than that baptism would be the ordinary means of regeneration."[83]

Again David's polemical skill is brought to bear. His opponents are held to say that since water in the Holy Scripture is frequently given as a symbol for the Spirit, that is the way in which John 3 should be interpreted. David counters by saying that it may well be that water is frequently so used. But if it were to be given that sense in this passage, it would produce a ridiculous interpretation. For Jesus says, "unless a man be born of water and of the spirit ..." "Now if water is to mean spirit, why then would he add the word spirit? If the word water is to signify spirit, then it would be the same as if Christ had said, 'except a man be born of the spirit and of the spirit'—which would be ridiculous."[84]

But, of course, what Christ has done here, as David sees it—and surely he is right on this count!—is to connect water and Spirit, a point which David underscores by citing and commenting on a plethora of Biblical passages. And having made the Spirit-Baptism connection, he is able to connect the reality of Christian spiritual existence to the gifts given in Baptism and in this way uphold his contention that Baptism is indeed the ordinary means of nothing less than *regeneration*.

In this connection, however, David undertakes another polemical task; viz. to set the reality of Baptism as *the event of regeneration* over against the hyper-Protestant notion that as a Sacrament, Baptism "is not more than an emblem." He begins his discussion by noting that under the Mosaic dispensation, before the incarnation, the things present in the Gospel were not immediately present but future. Therefore, types or emblems were appropriate. They indicated what was not yet there. But under the New Testament, such are inappropriate—indeed, radically wrong!—because the substance of the promise is now present. Therefore, to make an emblem under the New Testament is nothing less than idolatry, because emblems by necessity refer to a God other than the God of the Gospel, since the God of the Gospel is present in His now-fulfilled promises. There is nothing to pre-figure in the New Testament dispensation.[85]

In fact, as far as David is concerned, this talk of emblems only means that the "veil of Moses" still covers their hearts. And what is more, it results in the undoing of the Reformation.

> Now to make emblems in divine worship of those things that are present in reality, must be a notorious breach of this command [i.e. the First Commandment, so read as to include the prohibition of images] and a pagan idolatry. In vain protestants condemn the papish image worship, when they themselves turn the sacraments into images in their most solemn worship. Is not this the language of many protestants who deride the papists—baptism is an emblem of some spiritual gift! Bread and wine are holy emblems of Christ's body and blood![86]

Moreover, those who call Baptism an emblem end up teaching two Baptisms; an inward Baptism with the Holy Spirit and an outer "emblematic" Baptism. But, says David, this expressly contradicts the teaching of the apostolic Scripture which says, "one Lord, one faith, one baptism." And this one Baptism, he continues, is of water and the Spirit. Again, the polemical turn cannot be resisted and David wonders, if there are two Baptisms, why not two Lords and two faiths?[87]

To strengthen his case, David considers what seems to have been an objection, viz. the case of Cornelius in Acts 10. Here, it would seem, is a person who believed and received the Holy Spirit prior to, and so in effect without, the water. But as David evaluates things, "there is a difference between the faith in Christ yet to come and the faith in Christ already come."[88] And Cornelius, when he first appears in the narrative, is a believer in the Christ yet to come; i.e. he believes under the old dispensation. And, further, in his case the gift of the Spirit was miraculous and as such is not necessary to salvation. In fact, if Cornelius had God's entire salvific gift via the miraculous, why was he baptized at all? The very fact that he was baptized, in spite of the miraculous, demonstrates to David just how high is the dignity of this Baptism that is oft times demeaned with the epithet "water Baptism." In fact, David, concludes, the baptismal "putting on of Christ is far more valuable" than all the miraculous gifts! For the miraculous gifts are not necessary to salvation, but Baptism is.[89]

In his fifth section, David continues his discussion of the notion that Christ is put on in Baptism. This expression, he maintains, derives from a Roman custom of putting a new garment on a freed slave. In the case of Baptism, this means being clothed with all of Christ's merits: wisdom, righteousness, sanctification and redemption. Therefore, when the Father looks upon us wearing this new garment, He can only see His own beloved Son with whom He is pleased. In Christ, our sins are not merely pardoned, they are washed away, which is to say that Baptism effects not only pardon but sanctification and therefore it must be "in the fullest sense" the means of regeneration.[90]

David recognizes, of course, that there are some who think that the fact that people sin after Baptism calls such teaching into question. However, for David, the real solution to this problem lies in the way in which Baptism is actually to be used in the event of preaching. In the hands—better, in the mouth!—of the preacher, Baptism is, on the one hand, "an unspeakable consolation" to the despondent and despairing, while, on the other hand, it is a call to repentance to those who abuse the legacy of their Baptism.[91]

In order to display just how Baptism accomplishes its saving work, David now undertakes a careful exegesis of 1 Peter 3:20-21, which reads, according to his received translation, "Eight souls were saved by water. The like figure whereunto even baptism doth also now save us (not the putting away of the filth of the flesh, but the answer of a good conscience toward God.) by the resurrection of Jesus Christ." The flood, says David, like Baptism, consisted of water. This water, which destroyed others, upheld the ark. Without the ark, the flood would not have been saving. Likewise, in Baptism, for the water to be saving, something must be attached; viz. the Holy Spirit. This is accomplished by virtue of the fact that Baptism is performed in the name of the Trinity.

What is now achieved in this Trinitarian Baptism is described by Peter as "the answer of a good conscience toward God."

The English word "answer" represents the Greek term *Eperotema*, which, says David, indicates a "counter-question." This, he continues, has reference to a procedure in Roman commercial law.

> It was customary among the Romans, that when anyone bound himself in a reciprocal stipulation to another one before a court, he employed certain forms of questions; whereupon the other one was constrained immediately to impart his prescribed answers, otherwise the bargain was considered invalid. This was called *Eperotema*. Agreeably to this, there are also stipulations made in baptism. There are reciprocal questions and answers. In short, there is a covenant established, ... God and the baptized are in covenant ; ...
>
> Now who is it that puts forth the first question, that makes the first stipulation? It is not the sinner, for 'there is none that seeketh after God,' Rom.3,11. The sinner has not chosen Christ, but Christ him, John 15,16. God seeks the sinner, he stipulates to him the overtures of salvation. ... But the sinner must also ask God to perform his engagements sealed in baptism.[92]

Next, in section six, David establishes the connection between the covenant which is ratified in Christ and the covenant that God made with Abraham. In Christ, we are received into this Abrahamic covenant. Therefore, "to be circumcised in Christ" and "to be baptized into Christ" are synonymous terms. And the content of this Covenant is Christ Himself. It is Christ who is promised; Christ who is the resurrection and the life.[93]

Nowhere in the treatise does David undertake to present a sustained defense of the practice of baptizing infants, a lack which David recognizes in an end note and attributes to the prescribe limits of the treatise.[94] However, in this section which brings together the covenant with Abraham and its ratification in Christ we do receive a glimpse of what such a defense might look like. For David makes the point that as soon as it is recognized that "baptism seals the Abrahamic covenant," it would have to be recognized that infants are to be baptized since they were included in the Abrahamic covenant and its seal, before the coming of Baptism, i.e. circumcision, was applied to infants.[95]

The seventh and final section of *Heavenly Flood...* is a sustained argument of the case that by holy Baptism we are united with Christ in His death, burial and resurrection. The evidence is provided by exegesis of Romans 6:3-5. "Justification is connected with Baptism and sanctification is the blessed consequence." So David begins his case.[96] And this provides him with an immediate occasion to taunt the Baptists. In their "emblematic" approach, they say that Paul's connection between Baptism and burial with Christ proves that Baptism is to be done by immersion. But why, asks David, should the burial alone be represented when we are united not merely with His burial but with His life death and resurrection? But if we were to have an "emblematic" Baptism in all its dimensions, we would need an emblem for each part and in this case "I do not know whether all popedom can afford ceremonies superstitious enough to make all this emblematic nonsense."[97] David's point, bottom line, is that Baptism is no representation at all, but a union and this is not dependent upon symbols, but upon the Word.

> The text [Romans 6] does not say that Christ's death is represented by baptism, but we are baptized into his death. The very design of the text indicates that we must really be connected with Christ, with his death and burial. Why so? ans. The apostle expressly requires of all the baptized, because they were baptized into Christ's death etc. to walk in newness of life. Now how could the apostle require the walk of a new life of those who were baptized, if they were not new? A man must first be a new man, and possess a new life, before he can walk in a new life. ... If they were only emblematically baptized into Christ ... then their walk in a new life would also be only emblematical. Now what man of good sense would contend that we should only have an emblematic new life? Now the effect cannot be greater than the cause ... [I]t is impossible that an emblem should produce anything but an emblem. In this manner the base hypocrite may also be holy, for he can have an emblematical but not a real holiness. Christian people ought to shudder at ever calling baptism an emblem; for the conclusions are too ridiculous and blasphemous, which follow from such absurdities."[98]

David also challenges the notion that Baptism only initiates us into the visible Church, or as he hears it put, "baptism is the door to the visible church," which, he says, is why those who deny that Baptism is the means of regeneration, nevertheless continue to administer it. But even though this opinion is "imbibed by many" (including supposed Lutherans?), David contradicted it and carried out the contradiction as follows:

a) The Scriptures do not call Baptism the door to the Church. Christ is the door and,

b) through Him we get into the Church.

c) Through Baptism we get into Christ for we were baptized into Christ; into His death.

d) It is Christ, not the Church, who died for us. Therefore,

e) "we are brought by baptism into the Lord Jesus himself, into his death and burial, and now we also rise with him. O what happy news this is to the baptized!"

f) We are, of course, brought into the Church. But that nothing more than this is effected through Baptism, without being first initiated into Christ, this is what David denies and contradicts.[99]

Finally, David's positive statement on Baptism goes like this:

1. We are baptized into Christ's death and thus considered as if we had ourselves died. The death of Jesus is the foundation of justification and all subsequent blessings. Since His death is the satisfaction of the Law, it is the same as if we had rendered satisfaction ourselves. We are, therefore, free from the Law because the Law exacted the full punishment. The Law is thus annulled because it is satisfied. It has no further punishment to inflict.

We inherit our sin from Adam—a creature. We inherit life from Christ—the Creator.

Since Christ was crowned with glory and honor, so are we.
Since Christ destroyed the devil and delivered from hell, so are we.

"Satan may indeed tempt and sift, but he cannot conquer you ... But what a shame it is that great numbers with this prerogative are willing subjects of Satan!"[100]

His death merited the Spirit, therefore we get the Spirit.

2. We were buried with Christ into His death by Baptism; therefore all our sins are covered like a dead man in a grave. "If they

are buried they are not to be remembered any more."[101]

3. By Baptism, we also rise with Christ into a new life. In His resurrection, Christ will outlive His enemies. If we were planted with Him, we shall also be like Him in His resurrection. "If the life of Christ be endless, thou canst also have an endless life with Him."[102]

While *Heavenly Flood of Regeneration*, in spite of its polemical bite, was intended for Lutheran consumption and edification, it ended up providing an occasion to defend Lutheran doctrine against the frontier revivalism that surrounded the essentially rurally located Tennessee Synod. Soon after its publication, it was attacked by a Methodist revival preacher named Joseph Moore and in 1825 David published his response: *Answer to Mr. Joseph Moore, The Methodist*. This time the family press in New Market took care of the printing and distribution.[103]

David's method of defense is a point by point citation from Moore's book and then a refutation of the charge that has been made against him therein. In the course of this defense, David not only has the opportunity to restate his teaching about holy Baptism, but, since Moore offers the opportunity to discuss other matters, these also are taken up.

At his polemical best, David subjects Moore's text to a withering analysis of the language that is designed to show either the falsity or the absurdity of the content, or both. An extended citation from the very opening paragraphs of the book is a clear illustration of David at work.

> Mr. Joseph Moore in the preface to his strictures on my treatise says, that 'to every informed and unprejudiced mind it carried its own condemnation.' If this be correct, what need had he, to misrepresent the doctrines contained in it, for the purpose of giving them a refutation? A simple review of them, in their original colours, would have sufficed, to convince informed minds of their supposed futility. He on the first page, states, that I say, baptism is regeneration; and frequently asserts the same, in many other passages; and vehemently labours to prove that baptism cannot be regeneration; which tends to make my treatise appear ridiculous. But neither Mr. M. nor any other person ever saw in it, unless it was in a bewildered imagination, that baptism was regeneration. He nowhere pointed out the page, where

I said so: for this obvious reason; because he could not. I call baptism the ordinary means of regeneration: but who does not perceive the palpable difference, between the means of, and regeneration itself? ... [H]e in a clandestine manner asserts that I say 'baptism is regeneration or a heavenly flood of regeneration.' Why is the expletive conjunction Or here introduced? This is to insinuate that a heavenly flood of regeneration is the same as regeneration itself. This betrays either ignorance, or else willful perversion. The rules of grammar ought to teach any common English scholar, that a flood of regeneration, is not the same as regeneration itself. When I say, 'the mother of a child,' any person knows that I do not mean that the mother is the child. 'Flood of regeneration' is a similar phrase, is parsed in the same manner; and implies nothing more than a flood, which as a means, is to effect regeneration. ... Why does he attempt to impress his readers with the false idea that I teach baptism is regeneration? Is he no scholar? Does he as a Christian, and a Methodist minister, not venerate the truth? He must, in the very commencement, have despaired of his pretended refutation; otherwise he would not have taken his refuge to a glaring falsehood: by saying that I teach, baptism is regeneration! Did he think, that his readers, were so ignorant, that they could not perceive the difference, between the means of and regeneration itself?[104]

In the course of his refutation of "Mr. M." (as he regularly refers to his opponent), David is pressed to defend Lutheran doctrine against many of the charges that have been laid against it by *Schwaermerei* from the very beginning of the Lutheran movement. Early on, for example, David deals with the charge that Lutherans teach "consubstantiation," a doctrine which is said to differ "but very little from the papish doctrine of transubstantiation."[105]

It is, of course, interesting to see this charge raised with respect to holy Baptism, rather than the Lord's Supper. But Mr. Moore has made the charge because of two features of David's exposition of holy Baptism: viz. his establishing of the close connection between the Word of God, the Spirit of God and the water; and his identification of the Name of God and God Himself.[106] As he interprets these statements, Mr. Moore makes use of a common definition of his day. Consubstantiation means, "to be of the same substance, kind or nature; existence of more than one in the same substance, etc." And from this he draws the conclusion: "From the above definitions it appears that consubstantiation is the connecting and uniting of two natures, beings, or things together, so as to form one; or so as to exist together as one."[107]

In refuting the charge, David begins by leaning on the Augsburg Confession, confident that in it true Lutheran teaching is to be found. He provides his own translation of Article X: "Of the Lord's Supper, we teach thus: that the true body and blood of Christ, are truly present, administered and received in the Lord's supper, under the figure of bread and wine; wherefore the contrary doctrine is rejected."[108]

There is a "manifest difference", says David, between "being present and administered under the figure..." and "uniting ... so as to become one with them..." The difference with respect to the Sacrament of holy Baptism is for David to be found in the term "vehicle." "I called the water in baptism a vehicle of the command of Christ and the name of the Holy Trinity."[109]

Just what David means with the term "vehicle" is easily seen by means of the biblical evidence which David cites in support of his position. First, there are a series of passages from the Hebrew Bible: Exodus 3:2, "That the Lord appeared unto him in a flame out of the midst of the bush"; Exodus 34:5, "the Lord descened (sic) in the cloud, and stood with him there, etc."; Psalm 104:3, where it is said that the Lord makes "... the clouds his chariot," and walks "...upon the wings of the wind." On this basis, David concludes, "where can be the inconsistency when I call water in baptism, and the elements in the eucharist, the blessed clouds in which God descends to act and commune with sinners?"[110]

But there are also New Testament passages that David brings to bear on the issue. These passages all assert the indwelling of God or the Spirit of God in Believers (2 Corinthians 6:16; Galatians 4:6; 1 Corinthians 6:17 and 19 are all cited). These passages lead David to conclude, "It is evident that God may dwell in and operate on a saint; and yet not become one substance. Hence, if so, why can the spirit not be connected with the water of baptism, without being consubstantiated with the same? If Mr. M. reasons consistently, he must also deny, that God dwells in the saints, or that they are influenced by the Holy Spirit; because according to his statements, God and the saints would become one substance ..."[111]

And then, ratcheting up the polemic still higher he asserts, "Whether Mr. M. formally denied the influence of the spirit, I do not assert. Such as argue against Lutherans, impeaching them with the doctrine of consubstantiation because they maintain that the elements in the Lord's supper are connected with the body and blood; and the water in baptism with the spirit, perhaps do not know, that they are laying the very foundation, for denying the dwelling of God in his saints, and the influence of the spirit."[112]

And David goes on to show that Moore's argument finally turns against itself and the catholic consensus of the Church. Moore has asserted, quotes David, "It appears to me, agreeable to the doctrine of St. Paul, that the preaching of the Gospel is the ordinary means of regeneration; or the means by which people are enabled to believe on the Lord Jesus Christ, so as to be saved." And, continues David, "He also acknowledges, p.24 — that the spirit is connected with the word." But then David's analysis goes on:

> Preaching is performed with the lungs, and the organs of speech, with the assistance of air; hence the spirit would as much be substantiated with the words that flow from the preacher's lips, as with the water in baptism. What can be the difference, whether I believe the spirit is connected with the words that are formed by the organs of speech and the air, or that he is connected with water. ... So that, in the same manner, in which he impeaches me with this doctrine, he holds it himself. But to speak the truth, neither the preaching, not the water is consubstantiated with the spirit; but they are mediums by which he operates.[113]

And, of course David will hold up the classic Chalcedonian Christology of Christ's two natures. "The Son of God," he offers, "does not only dwell in and operate upon the humanity, he assumed; but has become one with the same: for 'the Word was made flesh.'... Nevertheless, without any mixture or confusion of the two natures."[114] Thus we see that David teaches that just as the human and divine natures in Christ are not joined together so as to make some *tertium quid*, so in the Sacraments of holy Baptism and the Lord's Supper, the earthly and heavenly elements are joined in such a fashion that you can't have one without the other. Nevertheless there is here also neither mixture nor confusion.

Next David must deal with Moore's charge that he has made "a little water in baptism equal to God."[115] The passages from *Heavenly Flood of Regeneration* which have produced this charge are reproduced by David and they are as follows:

> "Holy Baptism owes its value, dignity, and majesty to the Saviour's command, and the name of the Holy Trinity, in which it is performed." "The command of Christ, and the name of the Holy Trinity, constitute the ground-work of baptism, and water is their vehicle. Now as valuable, as holy, as saving, and as venerable, as the name of God is, just so valuable, holy, saving and venerable is baptism; because that name is the ground-work thereof."
>
> "God's name in scripture is frequently put for himself; ..."
>
> "Baptism is very holy, because God's name, which is in it is holy ..."

But to use these passages as Moore has done is, in David's eyes, to miss the entire point. David has in fact used Luther to make the case that the media used by God have no particular significance in and of themselves. They are significant because of the use that God has made of them. Therefore, all that Moore has succeeded in doing is to argue that God does not work through media; an argument for which, says David, he has provided no proof.[116]

However, perhaps the most intriguing section of David's *Answer to Mr. Joseph Moore, The Methodist* is his discussion of the name of God. For in this section, the debate between David and Mr. Moore not only cuts to the center of the biblical revelation of God, but pre-empts what has become a modern (or as it is often said, "post-modern") debate. The occasion for the debate is provided in the fact that David has baldly stated that in Holy Scripture "The name of God [is] the same as God himself."[117] But for Mr. Moore, such an assertion absurd.

Here, Mr. Moore turns out to represent the "post modern" critics of Christian biblical theological language. He says, "This [i.e.

the assertion that the name of God is the same as God himself] seems very strange to me, for I had always understood that names & things were different — that the name was one thing and the being or thing it represents was another — but Mr. H. unites them together, and makes them one and the same; which is contrary to fact."[118]

Indeed, for Moore, the naming of things is arbitrary, a matter of convenience. Names are used "by general consent" to point things out and they do not possess the nature or being of their referent. From this gap between the name and that to which it refers, Moore draws two conclusions; they might be seen as head and tale of a common coin. First, "the supreme being among us is called God, Lord, Jehovah, etc; among the Jews, I AM or Jehovah; among the Greeks Theos; among the Latins Deus, etc. But these names are not the Supreme Being himself; if they were, there would be as many supreme beings as there are names given."[119] Second, "The same name is often given to different beings without altering their nature, or changing them into other beings."[120]

Once again, for David, Moore just misses the point. What he has said may well be true when it is applied to creatures, but it does not apply to God! And here it is God with whom we are dealing. Therefore, says David, "This argument is not agreeable to the rules of logick; for it has more in the conclusion, than what is contained in the premises. ... Things and beings in general, constitute his premises, and God, who bears no analogy to any thing is brought into the conclusion; which all amounts to a sophism." In fact, David continues, were we to allow Moore's argument, we would have to concede to the Unitarians that since three men or beings cannot be one, the three divine persons cannot be one God.[121]

David then turns to the Scriptural witness to demonstrate the lack of analogy between creatures and God. "It is not true, that God has derived his name by common consent, like men do; for he has *revealed* his own proper name to Moses, calling himself I AM that I AM. ... Again, although men may have names, and not possess the nature and properties, which those names imply; yet this is not the case with God; for he in reality possesses all, his name implies."[122]

Further, David points out that Moore's argument of the range of words and names for God in various languages in no way implies, according to David's identification of name and person, many gods. "Does not Mr. M. plainly see that it is the same name, only in different languages? He might as well argue: a man in English is man; in Latin, Vir; in Greek Aneer; therefore it cannot be the same man."[123]

But David's defense is not merely negative. He has a series of positive assertions to make as well. In the first place, he shows that even if a human being's name is an arbitrary designation, it does, after all, become his proper name and is "peculiar to his person." Thus, "When a judge passes sentence of death against any culprit, he does it by naming him; but not only the representation of the culprit; but his person is to be executed. This shews that a man's name in law, is the same as his person. ... Hence the absurdity of names being representations of men."[124]

But this applies *a fortiori* with respect to God. For it is true, that a man does have his name by arbitrary designation and so it is not "so peculiarly himself" as God's name is God himself. God originally possesses in himself, what his name implies." David then goes on to list a series of terms in Hebrew and Greek (here transliterated) along with their translated English equivalents and maintains that all of the "perfections" or attributes in those terms are really possessed by God himself. The designations, that is, are not arbitrary. Nor for that matter is the name of "Jesus." As with the designations of God, the name "Jesus" includes all His divine perfections and mediatorial character.[125]

But David went on to show how Mr. Moore's logic finally turns against him! He focused his attention on Moore's notion that, since names only "represent" persons or beings, then it must be that God's name "represents" God. But if that it true, says David, then the name of God—remember that it is, according to Moore an arbitrary human designation that we are dealing with!—must fall under the stricture of the first commandment. "But to worship God's name, which according to Mr. M. is not God himself, but only his representation, would ... be idolatry; for assuredly an image used in worship, is a teacher of lies; it represents to us, that the eternal God is similar to something which is created."[126]

But in order to oppose Moore even more vigorously, David holds his argument up against the Scripture. He does this by taking a series of passages which use the phrase "the name of God/the Lord" and in each case placing Moore's term "representation" in its place. This will allow the reader, he says, to perceive the "impropriety" of Moore's critique. A few from David's list will make the point clear enough.

"For whosoever shall call upon the name (representation) of God shall be saved." (Romans 10:13) (Note that the biblical text reads name of the Lord.)

"Wherefore God has highly exalted him and given him the name (representation) which is above every name (representation); ..." (Phi. 2:9)

"Neither is there salvation in any other name (representation) under heaven given among men whereby we must be saved." (Acts 4:12)

David's intention in all these cases is clear. He wants to show that in the biblical usage, name and representation are not equivalent terms and that when the name of God is mentioned there accrues to it things which can only be connected with the reality of God. "All of this," he maintains, "is sufficient to prove that the name of God is God himself."[127]

In the sixth section of this little book, David undertakes to critique Moore's separation of the work of the spirit from the "external" means of grace. According to David, Moore's position is that "the blessings [which make the means effectual] are not contained in the means, but immediately proceed from God."[128] But, says David, to take this position is to deny that the blessings are contained in the Gospel Word, which is the same as "denying the divine authenticity of the holy scriptures; for if the word must first receive this blessing, it is then not already the word of God. . . . Such a word is nothing but an empty sound."[129]

But for David, such a position is the end of all pastoral ministry and all true hope for sinners. "For if the divine blessing be not contained in the word, they must either hear it in vain, or else be excused for not believing it."[130] David expands his case by comparing and contrasting three positions. The first, which he defines as "the Calvinists" posits a "secret decree of unconditional wrath" which results in a notion of "two calls": a common call and an effectual call. The common occurs in the outward Word of the Gospel, which all may hear, but which contains no divine blessing capable of regenerating a sinner. The effectual call, however, is only for the elect and is not necessarily connected to the Word. David assumes that Moore, as a Methodist, rejects such a position.

The second position, says David, is that the sinner can merit the favor of God by righteous works, "without receiving any unmerited gifts by the means." The third position, David's own, makes an intrinsic connection between the blessing and the means, a connection with makes the means in their faithful use salvific. But since the means are God's own gifts, their use cannot constitute a source of merit. Since this is the position that Moore denies, and since he is not a Calvinist, he finally "pleads up that most absurd doctrine, that a sinner can merit salvation by legal works."[131]

David, however, will not stop with showing the inherent works righteousness of the position that separates the effective divine blessing from the external Word of the Gospel's proclamation. He goes on to argue that those who minister such an empty word are not worthy of being supported in such a ministry, for they in fact give nothing in return for their support. In fact they have by their own definition no reason to exist!

> In vain the clergy, with the garb of sanctity, who maintain this position, exhort their people, to contribute for the purpose of educating young men for the ministry, and sending them out as missionaries; and extort extravagant salaries, to support themselves and their families; not unfrequently (sic) in the luxuries of high life? When they administer nothing but an outward ineffectual gospel, and sacraments without a substance; so that poor people, notwithstanding this pious parade, must yet with agonizing suspense, wait for this secret effectual calling, which their priests tell them without a blush, is not to be had in such outward things, as the gospel word and sacraments, which they administer. Such a ministry is a pest to and a most gross imposition on society; for it is robbing the people of their temporal substance; when in exchange they receive no spiritual gifts, unless it be rarely one of the favourite elect, who receives a secret call, or one who by his works merits heaven; whereas all the rest, for want of this supernatural something must be damned forever.[132]

How different that is, argues David, from the true Gospel ministry, about which Christ said, "He that heareth you heareth Me." When this ministry is exercised, "...we have no need to wait for another call, or view our salvation at a great distance; for 'the word which we preach is nigh thee, even in thy mouth and in thy heart; that is, the word of faith which we preach; ...'"[133]

Further, David continues, the separation of the Spirit from the Word opens the door to the abuse of the Holy Scriptures. The door is opened to "private interpretation," whether by pope or Pietist and treats the Bible as a written revelation that cannot be depended upon.[134]

David, of course, knows that there are parables and metaphors in Scripture; that is to say, symbolic language. But for him these symbols are not esoteric. Their signification is to be sought in their context. And if the meaning is still not clear, the interpreter does better to exercise patience and await the result of further study than "invent a meaning, which you conceive to be rational or with which inspired you suppose to be inspired."[135]

III

In September of 1826, The Tennessee Synod meeting in Sullivan County Tennessee undertook to meet the rising threat of American Unitarianism. To meet the threat, David Henkel was requested to write a book on the Divinity of Christ. Two years later, David was able to report that he had finished the work. It was not until 1830, however, that book was printed, and that only after David had died earlier in the year. The title page includes the notation, "Published by order of The Evangelical Lutheran Tennessee Synod." Thus the book was taken out of the realm of the personal and made a part of the public teaching of the church body.[136]

The book itself, focusing on the writing and preaching of a certain Unitarian clergyman, James Miller, is divided into six sections. The first section is intended to refute the Unitarian charge that there is no difference between three divine persons and three divine beings, in other words, that Trinitarian faith is really tri-theism.

"That God is but one being is admitted by all Christian denominations, and also by Mehometans, Deists and Devils."[137] So David begins his riposte. The issue for debate, therefore is not the unity of God's *being*, but the Trinity of His persons. In this respect, the Unitarians go wrong in their argument because they fail to distinguish between *being* and *person*. Miller had argued that being and person are "the same, or terms of synonymous signification." But David sees this as being based on a confusion of uses. Miller, he says, has used Scripture to show that *human beings* and *human persons* are synonymous. But David then, in similar fashion to his rebuttal of Moore, contends that when Scripture uses the word "person" with respect to God it does not mean the same thing as when the reference is with respect to created beings. And when referred to God, the words undergo a transformation.

David asks, "Is it congenial to correct logic to conclude that the mode of God's existence is like that of man? ... In reasoning on the being and relations of God, it would be absurd to confound Him with anything that is created, or to illustrate His character in this manner ..." And then David adds the obvious proviso, "... unless He Himself has indicated the clue in the scripture."[138]

Here is a major point in the matter of hermeneutics. Granted the Bible's language is analogous, the analogies are controlled by God, not the human interpreter and so must be used according to their divinely determined intent, if they are to be used correctly. Therefore, to show that the Trinity is absurd is not a matter of proving that three human beings cannot be one man, but of proving, rather, that the Trinity "is repugnant to *God's* essence, character, attributes and relations ..."

In the effort to show a correct usage of biblical language David refers to the following from Hebrews 1:3; "...Who being the brightness of His glory and the express image of his person..." And he draws the following conclusion:

> If Christ be the brightness of the Father's glory, then the Father Himself must be a light; for a brightness supposes a light. God in the Scripture is called a light, a fire, a sun ... As the nature of the light is, so is the nature of its brightness.
>
> A created light reflects a created brightness, but an uncreated light reflects an uncreated brightness. God is an eternal, uncreated light, Christ is the brightness of His glory, consequently Christ is eternal and uncreated. The brightness of a light is also truly light, yet distinguished from the light by which it is reflected. Or properly the brightness of the luminary is the luminary itself reflected. Christ is the brightness of God's glory, God is a light a sun, hence Christ is God reflected.[139]

For David, this puts the Unitarians in a dilemma. Either they must suppose that a brightness can be separated from its luminary so as to constitute a distinct substance, which is wrong—David would say "contrary to fact"—or they must deny that Christ is the brightness of the Father's glory, which would be contrary to Scripture, "the declaration of God's word."

David does two things in this argument. First, he applies a rigorous logical analysis to both his material and the Unitarian objection. This is not a know-nothing traditionalism posed against "reason." Second, he argues his case biblically. Of course, Mr. Miller has invited this. Modern day Unitarians wouldn't care.

David continues his argument by making use of Isaiah 42:8, "I am the LORD; that is my name; and my glory will I not give to another, neither my praise to a graven image." Since Christ is the glory of God in the reflecting of it, David concludes that "he is by no means a separate *being* from his Father," otherwise, God would be sharing His glory with another.[140]

David employs a similarly rigorous evaluation with respect to any number of key biblical predicatives of God and/or Christ in order to show that they make their sense only if we treat them in terms of relationships that are unifying rather than separating. For instance, he refers to the expression, in Hebrews 1:3, KJV, "the express image of his person." The Greek word here rendered "express image," properly indicates an impression made by a stamp; while the Greek word translated in this place as "person" properly means a reality, a substance or an existence. Thus David concludes, "Christ is the impression of God's substance, hence God's own substance, or existence is perfectly impressed in him; so that the Father is in and identified with his person: for he saith: 'he that hath seen me hath seen the father.'"[141]

But perhaps nowhere is David's penetrating logic on display more than when he deals with the biblical expression that God is light. It is obvious, David argues, that is impossible for a light to exist without its brightness. Rather, it is the very nature of light to have brightness. But since God is uncreated light, so His brightness must likewise be an uncreated brightness. Moreover, the brightness of a light is not a product of the will of a light, as if it might have been left in non-existence. If there is a light, then there is a brightness. But since God's existence is not contingent but absolute, His brightness must also be absolute and not contingent, even if it is *"dependent."*[142]

David also argues that the whole of the Unitarian critique misses the Trinitarian point. His opponent, Miller, has argued that the Scriptures use the terms "Father" and "God" synonymously and that therefore the Father is referred to as the "supreme" God. Having identified Miller's texts in this regard, David goes on to say that Miller has assumed that all these texts refer to the Father and then has used them to raise a series of questions: If the Father of Christ is the highest (Luke 1:32), the eternal (Psalm 91:9), the living God (Genesis 14:18), the invisible God (Deuteronomy 33:27), the only true God (John 17:3), the only wise God (Romans 16:27), Omnipotent (Revelation 19:6), without variableness or shadow of turning (James 1:17), can any of these things be said of any other, even Jesus Christ, whom Miller calls "The Son and Image of God"?[143] The implied answer is, of course, negative and therewith the Trinitarian doctrine is held to be repudiated.

But David responds by acknowledging that "no other being besides the Father can be the eternal God. ...," but he immediately continues, "... *nor is this the point in question.*" (Italics added.) What, then, is the controversy about? "Whether or not the Father and Christ are one being." Which is to say that Mr. Miller is guilty of dealing with the Trinitarian persons when he should be dealing with the unity of being. David returns to his light/brightness analogy: "Suppose I were to say that the sun was the only luminary of day to the exclusion of all others and then concluded that hence the brightness thereof could not be light, should I not be exploded?" "Is not Christ the brightness of God's glory? If so, is he not one being with the father?"

The point is that since Christ is one with the Father, He who is the Son of God is God, the Son, just as the brightness emitted by the sun is the sun's own brightness and not that of another luminary. Nevertheless, Christ also sustains another relationship to the Father. He is the mediator and in this regard is distinct from the Father. Thus, when the Unitarians cite John 17:3, "This is eternal life, that they might know Thee, the only true God and Jesus Christ whom Thou hast sent," they miss the point that what is here distinguished is sender and sent, mediator and mediated, not divine being and some other sort of being.[144] The passage is just not to the Unitarian point. Moreover, the very thing that is here ascribed to God, viz. that eternal life is to know God, is in this very place ascribed to Jesus Christ; which would, of course, be an argument for the unity of being.

Similar treatments are given to the theme of God's invisibility and Christ's visibility, holiness, immortality and others. In every instance, the issue for David Henkel revolves around the fact that in Holy Scripture divine attributes are predicated of Christ, which is acknowledged by his opponents. (cf. footnote 144.) Such biblical sources require the attribution of divinity itself to Christ and therefore promote Trinitarian thinking rather than speak against it.

In the course of the discussion, David deals with the issue of the nature of theological language. He is at great pains to show that while words such as "father" and "son" are common human words, they are not used metaphorically of God, i.e. we do not proceed from what is known of human fathers and sons in some general way. Rather, the words are used analogously and we must be careful to observe just wherein the analogy exists. This means that the words, when applied to God, take on new meaning derived from the nature of God, to whom the words are now applied. Thus, there are some among David's opponents who want to apply the term "son" merely to Jesus' humanity. But since Jesus' humanity is the common humanity that he shares with all human creatures, and this humanity is "creature," this, says, David, would be to equate begetting with creating. This is, of course, just what happened with the Enlightenment, but David shows that even at the height of the Enlightenment's influence, serious Trinitarian thinking was able to argue the Bible's case coherently.[145]

But David is interested in just why this confusion between begetting and creating has been made in the first place. And his answer is that it happens because his Unitarian opponent has forgotten the factor of eternity. The activity of begetting (as well as that of the Holy Spirit's procession) does not take place in time. If so, then there would be an anteriority and a posteriority. But in the case of the Holy Trinity, begetting and proceeding are activities that occur within the eternal life of the Trinity and therefore without the implications of time.[146]

Since the Unitarians of early 19th century intended to be

biblical, a great deal of *David Henkel Against The Unitarians* is devoted specifically to biblical exegesis. In these arguments, David demonstrates his ability to handle the biblical texts with great sophistication; a sophistication that is hardly to be expected of one who was self taught. For now, a single example will have to suffice to illustrate his skill.

The issue at hand is the two natures Christology of the Council of Chalcedon. It has come into the discussion because the Unitarian opponents have brought it forward as "a main prop in the edifice of the trinity." They, of course, object to this Christology. And for more than one reason: In the first place they complain that "It represents [Christ] as speaking in two characters, sometimes as God, sometimes as man, without intimating in which character." But perhaps even more important theologically is the fact that they cannot square the humiliation of Christ with the notions of God's "immutable perfections and nature."

In response to this critique, David turns to the Bible. (Remember, these are "biblical" Unitarians who, it could be assumed, can be swayed by sound biblical evidence.) But for him it is not just a matter of citation, but of careful and extensive exegesis. His first text is Matthew 22:41–46—Jesus' question to the Pharisees concerning the relationship of the Christ to King David. Here, according to David's analysis, Christ is spoken of in a two-fold way. He is both King David's Lord and King David's son. As King David's son, He possesses King David's nature, which is a created nature and thus Christ is a true human being. But as King David's Lord, He must be superior to him. But what is the nature of this superiority, our David asks. And this he answers with reference to 1 Corinthians 15:47: "...The second man is the Lord from heaven."[147] David argues that the term "from heaven" here has the sense of "before creation," since even the Unitarians (as the Arians of old) agreed that God had created the world through Christ. But surely Christ must have had a nature prior to creation, otherwise He would be a non-entity. But this cannot have been His human nature, since He received that from King David, by virtue of being King David's son.[148]

But still, is this second nature divine? To further his argument, David turns to Romans 9:5: "...whose are the fathers and of whom, as concerning the flesh, Christ came, who is over all, God blessed for ever." (KJV) "It is vain," says our David, "to suppose that the phrase "God Blessed forever," has reference to the Father, implying a form of thanksgiving and that the substantive verb be ought to be understood; so that the sense would be: Christ is over all, therefore God the Father be blessed forever. Amen. This is not possible, he maintains (and here he clearly has a Greek text to work with!), because the original text reads θεος ευλογητος and ευλογητος is not a participle but an adjective. Unlike participles, adjectives do not imply time and hence it is not possible, according to correct grammatical usage to construe the phrase to mean "God be blessed forever." Rather, what is here said is that Christ is over all and thus Himself supreme God "for no being can be above all things; except God."[149] All of which is to say that as King David's Lord, the Christ is superior to King David with divine superiority.

Of course, David maintains that these two natures of Christ exist in a single unitary person and therefore, whether speaking or acting or being acted upon, it is the one God-Man who is involved. At just this point, David's argument takes an interesting twist; a twist that indicates just how sophisticated David's thinking was and how aware he was of the history of the Church's doctrine. For at just the point where the true unity of the two natures is involved, David turns his attention to "those Trinitarians who deny that the natures in Christ are so deeply and inseparably united that the properties of each (yet without mixture or confusion) flow together in the same person."[150] The "Trinitarians" whom David has in mind are Calvinists. And what David has in minds is their unwillingness to use the doctrine of the *communicatio idiomatum* in the radical Lutheran manner—an unwillingness that, according to David, plays into the hands of the Unitarians.

"Christ," says David, "is a personal appellation including two natures. But how was he the seed of David, when he had an eternal pre-existence? The Apostle says that he was of the seed of David according to the flesh. It is the property of the flesh to be derived from David; yet it is properly said that Christ is of the seed of David, because his flesh is one thing with himself: for the Word was made flesh; hence whatsoever may be the properties and actions of the flesh, the divine nature is a partaker of the same."

And this includes the suffering and death as well.

The flesh only is subject to mortality; whereas the

divine nature in itself is immortal. The human nature of itself possesses no quickening power; hence to quicken is a work peculiar to divine nature. Nevertheless the flesh and the divine nature are one person, consequently if the flesh died; the Godhead was a partaker of this death; because this flesh and blood is God's own flesh and blood. Heb.2:14; but also that 'God purchased his church with his own blood.' Acts 20:28[151]

David, pursuing his radical line of thought, claims that the Calvinist teaching presumes "that nothing more than the human nature died." Or again, "that a mere man died." And he continues, the Unitarian critique finds such teaching a vulnerable target. When his Unitarian opponent attacks that Calvinist Christology, "His arguments ... it must be confessed are cogent and conclusive. But it must be observed that not all Trinitarians maintain that a mere man suffered and died. Lutherans in particular disavow such an opinion. They believe that Christ, hence not a mere man, suffered and died."[152]

And David goes on to further censure this weak Christology as being guilty of contradiction and counsels that,

> If they cannot believe that the God-head of Christ could be a partaker of suffering and death, why do they not at once deny that he is God? ... Whatever Christ may be, the same must have been a partaker of sufferings and death. Was he a mere man, then a mere man only suffered and died. Was he a sublime spirit superior to any of the angels joined to a human body, then such a spirit was a partaker of suffering and death. Was he God reflected, or the brightness of the Father's glory made flesh, then this filial godhead suffered and died in the flesh.[153]

David further wants to know whether those Trinitarians who deny that God dies believe that Christ was God or a mere man while He was dead. If it is the former, then they must admit that His Godhead participated in the death. If it is the latter, then they must deny that He has the power to raise Himself from the dead.

At this point, David is willing to put his own position to the test. Rather than "raise Himself," would it not be more accurate, he asks to say that the *Father* raised Him? That is, of course, true, says

David. But it is not to be said to the exclusion of the former statement. For example, John 10:17 and 18 testify that Christ "laid down his life that he might take it again; he had the power to lay it down and He had the power to take it again." And John 5:19 affirms "The Son can do nothing of Himself, but what He sees the Father do; for whatever He does, these things the Son does likewise." Thus both statements are true.[154] The crowning statement of David's radical Christology then follows:

> Had the Godhead of Christ been separated from the humanity in death, then Godhead would have been a distinct person from the humanity; hence had the Godhead thus separated, even raised humanity, it could by no means be said that he raised Himself, but the Son of God would only have raised up a mere man with whom he at the time had no personal connection. But as the Scripture plainly shows that Christ raised Himself, he must have been God-man even in death. Can one be raised from the dead; provided he be not dead? By no means. Could a God-man have raised Himself provided a mere man but not a God-man had been dead? By no means. Since Christ raised Himself from the dead, it is evident that His Godhead, even in death, was not separated from his humanity.[155]

This argument, worthy of the great Fathers of the Church, not only speaks against the Christology of the "inconsiderate Trinitarians" who play into the Unitarian hands, as David sees it, but it also tells against the Unitarians of David's day. For these "biblical" Unitarians hold that the "fullness of Godhead dwells bodily in Christ" and that He is almighty and does His miracles by the indwelling of the Father. What they want to deny, together with the "inconsiderate Trinitarians," is that the Godhead was abased when Christ was. It is clear that the real stumbling block in the doctrine of the Trinity, a stumbling block which David was not about to let his opponents avoid, is the very nature of deity.[156] The traditional notion of Deity, which was inherited from the high Greek paganism, whose "theologians" were the classical philosophers (Plato and Aristotle, to name the most prominent), was that deity is unchangeable or immutable; even apathetic. But that doctrine is directly affronted by the proclamation of the abasement of Christ. If Christ is divine and actually abased, then the very notion of deity will have to be revised.

David's term for the divinity of Christ is "filial godhead," by which he means the person of the Son who has the Father's substance. Here David has recourse to what has been called, in the history of dogmatics, the "immanent Trinity," i.e., the persons of the Godhead in their relationships to one another. In this respect, David affirms, "...Christ is not His own God. The Father is called Christ's God." This is critically important for dealing with the passages of Holy Scripture which imply a split between Christ and God. For example, when Jesus cries out on the cross, "My God, My God! Why have You forsaken Me?," it should not be taken to mean that the Father was "personally out of Christ." Rather, it is the Father who appears to have forsaken the Son, both of whom are of the same divine substance. Indeed, the very notion of "to forsake does not always imply a local or personal separation." David asks—and the answer is implied in the asking—"God forsakes the wicked and leaves them to the hardness of their hearts; yet who can deny that they as well as others live, move and have their being in Him?"[157]

David also holds up an argument that once again has been made by both the Unitarians and "inconsiderate Trinitarians" to the effect that if the divine nature really suffered and died in Christ the entire universe would have collapsed. Once again, David's recourse is to the doctrine of the Trinitarian persons. It is the Son who became incarnate and suffered and died in the flesh, not the Father. And indeed, seen from that standpoint, the cosmic disasters at the time of the crucifixion demonstrate that this Crucified One must surely be the God-man and no mere man.[158]

A most interesting side light to David's theological acumen appears at this point. While David never "footnotes" his sources, he clearly has more at his disposal than would be expected from a frontier preacher; especially a frontier preacher with virtually no formal education. Here he quotes Dionysius the Areopagite, whom he describes as a "heathen philosopher." Moreover, he quotes the Areopagite in Latin and then produces his own translation for the benefit of his readers.

David is also the master of taking his opponents' arguments and turning them back on the opponents themselves. One of the major Unitarian arguments against the divinity of Christ is that

He could not be God because He said that He could do nothing by Himself. As David quotes their argument: "'If' say they, 'he had infinite power would it be true for him to say that he *could of himself do nothing?*'" Or again: "If the Son possessed in himself all fullness why should the Father have communicated any assistance to his humanity? Would he not have been personally sufficient of himself?"

But the argument actually works in the opposite direction for David. It is creatures who may exert their own abilities without an immediate exertion of omnipotence. Therefore, if Christ could do anything without the Father, it would follow that he, like all creatures, had a separate power and distinct being from the Father. But since He can do nothing of Himself but can only act in unity with the Father, it proves that he and the Father have the same uncreated power. Thus, the identity of power proves the identity of being.

David's text in this regard is John 5:19. "The Son can do nothing of Himself but what He seeth the Father do: for what things soever He doeth, these also doeth the Son like wise." (KJV) David offers the following comment on this text: "The Father performed works of omnipotence, Christ performed the same works; hence he must possess the same omnipotence. When two persons possess the self-same power, it is manifest that one cannot act with this power but only in conjunction with the other."[159]

A fundamental element of David's method is that the biblical vocabulary gains its precise meaning from its referent. Take for example, the term "everlasting" or "forever." David cites a long list of biblical passages in which the term means simply a long period of time. But the referent in all these cases is not God but the creature. And creatures exist in time. In David's analysis, "time" is not perduration, but quite the contrary it is the materia of progression, succession and change. Therefore, "everlasting" or "forever" will carry a temporal sense. But when the referent is God, it is another matter entirely. Since God exists prior to time, the term cannot have a temporal sense.

This argument produces two results for David. The first is that although "everlasting" or "forever" *can* have a temporal sense, the "can" does not prove that it either *must* or *does* have a temporal sense when the referent is Christ. Second, the biblical texts that give Christ a full role in the creation of the world (Hebrews, John 1, Proverbs) locate Christ in eternity, since time itself is a part of the created order. Therefore, with respect to Christ, the term must have an eternal reference. But then, it is precisely Trinitarian and not Unitarian teaching that preserves the biblical teaching of the *unity* of God.[160]

This latter point is a constant undercurrent throughout this little book. His Unitarians, because they attribute divine activity to Christ while denying His one being with the Father are really the ones who divide God's One-ness.

It is also interesting to see that David's defense of the Trinitarian doctrine of God means also a defense of the radical Lutheran Trinitarian doctrine against the milder, but more common Calvinist variety. In a final chapter of the book, entitled "The Incarnation of the Son of God," after summarizing his arguments, David directly takes up the challenge posed by the Reformed Christology, which David sees as playing into the hands of the Unitarians. Beginning, as a sound historian should, in the sacramental controversy between Luther and Zwingli, David lays out the difference between Lutheran and Reformed teaching is as stark a way as possible.

> Luther who maintained the omnipresence of Christ's body, hence the presence of His body and blood and in the Lord's Supper, believed that the person of the Word was made the person of the flesh; so that the humanity in this union, without confusion or a change of natures, is in possession of all divine attributes, and is therefore omnipotent, omnipresent, and an object of adoration.... Whereas Zuinglius, who denied the presence of the Lord's body and blood in the sacrament supposed that the humanity was not susceptible of receiving such divine dignity and glory, and that it is unreasonable to believe the omnipresence of Christ's body. Calvin also, and his followers maintained the same position.
>
> This is one of the principle points on which Lutheran and Calvinistic churches have been divided since the time of the Reformation. Lutherans according to their position, suppose that the humanity of Christ in union with the Word, is an object of religious worship. But Calvinists and German Reformed must necessarily according to their principles deny such worship to the Lord's humanity, and consider it idolatry. If Lutherans should err in this point

they must certainly be idolaters; but if Calvinists err they are in open opposition to Christ's glory in his mediatorial character, and deny him that honor which God requires men and angels to render unto him. Again, if the position of Calvinists should be correct, one of the strongest objections of Unitarians against the doctrine of Christ's Godhead will remain utterly unanswerable.[161]

In order to establish the accuracy of his description of the Calvinist/Reformed position, David cites Calvin, Theodore Beza, Peter Martyr, Palatine Kednadon, all of which he takes from a work of Lucas Osiander[162] as well as the Heidelberg Catechism.[163] In each of the former instances, he cites the Latin or German of his source and then provides his own translation.

To make the Lutheran case, he uses a Latin edition of the Book of Concord, citing from the the Formula of Concord's Christological article (VIII) in which Luther's own writings are giving confessional status. He again provides his own translation.

But David does more than merely cite a pair of opposing arguments from the past. He is concerned, rather, with making argument in support of the Lutheran doctrine in the present time. This means, for him, to affirm the personal presence of the God-Man, Jesus Christ, with His Church. And David really means the *man* element of that God-Man. If that were not so, there would be no difference between the relationship of divinity and humanity Christ and the presence of God with any believer. He argues:

> If Christ's divine nature were omnipresent without the humanity (as the Calvinist/Reformed position maintains); and yet, be personally united with the same, then it would follow that every saint was personally united to God: for God is united with and dwells in all believers; they indeed are located, whilst God united to them is omnipresent. But can this be called a personal union? Can it be said that God was made flesh in them? By no means. The Father and the Holy Ghost are also united to the humanity of Christ. ... But is the Father or the Holy Ghost personally united to the humanity of Jesus? Or was the Father or the Holy Ghost made flesh? By no means. Now since neither the Father nor the Holy

Ghost was made flesh, but the Son only, it must follow that the person of the Son is deeply united with the flesh; so that the flesh is wherever the Godhead may be. Thus it must be evident that the filial Godhead is more closely united to his flesh than the Father or the Holy Ghost and therefore exists nowhere without his assumed humanity."[164]

This explicit denial of the so-called *Extra Calvinisticum* is tightly argued on the basis of careful exegesis of Scripture and doctrinal logic of the Incarnation which shows that talk of the "presence of God" must be a two-fold affair. There is talk of the general omnipresence of God. But there is also talk of God's incarnational presence, in which case it is always the whole Christ, the one God-Man, who is the referent. "Is it not acknowledged by all that the Father is omnipresent? If Christ according to his humanity went to the Father, it is so far from proving that the same is not omnipresent that it establishes its omnipresence. For if Christ went to the Father then he must be wherever the Father may be, but the Father is omnipresent." Or again:

> When Christ ascended to heaven he was also exalted at God's right hand. ... If it be asked, according to which nature was Christ exalted at God's right hand? It must be answered, according to his human nature. It has already been shewn that he humbled himself according to this nature; for he was put to death in the flesh. ... And as this exaltation took place in consequence of his preceding humiliation, it is evident that the humanity was exalted....[from many Biblical passages here discussed] it is sufficiently manifest that the right hand of God is Almighty and omnipresent.[165]

In the end, however, as it has ever been in Lutheran circles, it is pastoral concern that guides David's proclamation of biblical truth. And therefore the concluding paragraphs of his book stake the claim.

> The text says that he ascended far above the heavens that he might fill all things. He that fills all things; hence the universe, must undoubtedly be omnipresent. By Christ's ascension he fills all things, which proves that by his exaltation he got the exercise of all dominion. His ascension

therefore, is so far from proving that he is not omnipresent, that it establishes his omnipresence. When Christ fills all things no place can be found where he is not present.

After Christ's glorious ascension St. John the Divine saw him in a vision walking in the midst of the seven candlesticks, i.e. in the midst of his church. He saw him as the Son of Man; for he describes his head, hair, eyes, feet, right hand &c. which are members indicating his human body ... Now when John saw the glorified body of his Jesus in the midst of the churches, it proves his omnipresence, and a knowledge of it proves a great consolation to all believers.[166]

IV

As the Church of Jesus Christ moves into the Third Millennium A.D., the Lutheran witness to the Gospel is at risk of serious compromise. Forces from the theological left and the theological right and new forces, such as the "Church Growth Movement" and "New Age Spirituality" threaten to make such inroads into the Lutheran Church that will at least becloud and more likely eradicate her unique witness to Christ and His Gospel. She will need all available resources to ward off the attack. One of those resources is the witness of her own theologians from past generations. Such witness is in serious need of retrieval. For Lutherans in America, the retrieval should surely include, perhaps begin with, the witness of the "Henkelites," and David Henkel chief among them.

The present volume, *David Henkel Against the Unitarians*, is issued as a contribution to this much needed effort.

Dr. Louis A. Smith
Waynesboro, Virginia

Endnotes

[1] I wish to thank Miss Karen Vest and the staff at the Waynesboro VA public library whose help in obtaining some rare documents has made even the gathering of materials for this essay a pleasure. Thanks also to Mr. Robert Carpenter of Bessemer City, North Carolina who also shared some valuable work of his own. Some of the material has appeared in "The Early Career of David Henkel". *Lutheran Quarterly*, vol. XVI, no.3, Autumn 2002. pp.302ff. We are grateful for their permission to use the material.

[2] Socrates Henkel, *History of The Evangelical Lutheran Tennessee Synod* (New Market, VA: Henkel & Co, 1890) 80f.

[3] Both the North Carolina Synod and the Tennessee Synod were officially described as "...Synod of North Carolina [or Tennessee] and Adjacent States."

[4] Socrates Henkel, *History of The Evangelical Lutheran Tennessee Synod* (New Market, Virginia: Henkel & Co., 1890) pp. 67f.

[5] G.D. Bernheim, *History of the German Settlements and of the Lutheran Church in North and South Carolina* (Philadelphia: Publisher, 1875) 366.

[6] Synods in Ohio, Indiana, Kentucky and Illinois owed their beginnings to the Henkels in one way or another.

[7] Letter from David Henkel to his Brother Solomon, dated Dec.20, 1820. Miller Collection. The Handley Regional Library, Winchester, VA. In this letter, David is soliciting Solomon's help in obtaining charcter references and specifically requests one form his former teacher

[8] The endorsement from William Hill of Winchester, VA is to be found in the Collection of David Henkel Papers in the Gettysburg Seminary library.

[9] Letter from John Dreher to Solomon Henkel, November 10, 1812. Henkel Family Papers, University of Virginia Special Collections, 8653-d. Box 1

[10] W, Eisenberg, *The Lutherans in Virginia* (Salem, VA: Virginia Synod, LCA, 1967) p.123.

[11] Klaus Wust, *The Virginia Germans* (Charlottesville, VA: University of Virginia Press, 1965) 132f.

[12] From the beginning, David seems to have exceeded the literal description of a catechist, in that he produced the sermons that he read.

[13] Peschau. North Carolina Synod Minutes, (South Carolina: Kreider, 1835) Pages.

[14] The letter, dated December 13, 1813 and postmarked January 15, 1814, is found in the Henkel Papers, University of Virginia Special Collections, Charlottesville, VA. 8653-C. Box#1

[15] ibid.

[16] The standard biography of Shober, *Gottlieb Shober of Salem*, is by Jerry Surrat (Macon, GA. Mercer University Press. 1983)

[17] Peschau p.24f.

[18] The letters from Miller to Shober are preserved in the North Carolina Lutheran Synod Archives in Salisbury, NC.

[19] Paul Henkel. *Der Christliche Catechismus*. New Market, VA. S. Henkel's Druckerei. 1816.

[20] Lewis Mayer to Solomon Henkel, February 16, 1812 & John Ravenscroft to Solomon Henkel, July 16, 1818 and September 16, 1818. The Henkel Collection,

University of Virginia Special Collections, 8653-d Box #1.

[21] Peschau p.28. cf. Socrates Henkel. *History of The Evangelical Lutheran Tennessee Synod.* New Market, VA, The Henkel Press. 1890. p.11

[22] Petitions from the White haven Congregation, August 26, 1916, the Cabins Creek Congregation, October 2, 1816 and the Lebanon Congregation, October 11, 1816 are preserved in the North Carolina Lutheran Synod Archives in Salisbury, NC.

[23] Peschau p.29. This odd circumstance seems to be at the root of the trouble indicated in the Miller letters. cf. above footnote 15.

[24] David Henkel Diary. Typescript in North Carolina Synod Archives. p.15

[25] Committee on Historical Work, *Life Sketches of Lutheran Ministers* (Columbia, S.C.: North Carolina Synod, LCA, 1966) p.127f.

[26] The dating here lends itself to two possible interpretations. David was aware, prior to the meeting of Synod that he would be granted the privilege of ministering in all the congregations, or, having made the commitments without permission, the granting of the privilege pulled his chestnuts from the fire.

[27] David Henkel to Gottlieb Shober, letter of March 17, 1817. North Carolina Synod Archives, Salisbury, N.C.

[28] Jerry L. Surratt, *Gottlieb Shober of Salem* (Macon, GA: Mercer University Press, 1983) pp. 150ff.

[29] M. Geiger. "Jung-Stilling," *Die Religion in Geschichte und Gegenwart.* Dritte Auflage. Tuebingen. J.C.B. Mohr (Paul Siebeck). 1957. Band 3 pp. 1070–1071.

[30] David Henkel. *The Essence of the Christian Religion.*

[31] The copy of the *Essence of the Christian Religion* available to me carries no page numbers. Neither is the date of publication indicated.

[32] Ibid.

[33] Shober to David Henkel, March 23, 1815. in the Miller Collection, The Handley Regional Library, Winchester, VA.

[34] David Henkel. *Loud Trumpet of Futurity: or A Few Reflections on Future Things.* Salisbury, N.C. Jacob Krider. 1817.

[35] R. J. Miller to Shober, July 15th, 1817. North Carolina Synod Archives, Salisbury, NC.

[36] G.D. Bernheim. *History of The German Settlements and of The Lutheran Church in North and South Carolina.* Philadelphia. The Lutheran Bookstore. 1872. pp.395 ff. cf. Peschau's Minutes for these years.

[37] cf. Socrates Henkel. *History of the Evangelical Lutheran Tennessee Synod,* p.15

[38] cf. David Henkel, *Carolinian Herald of Liberty; Religious & Political.* Salisbury, N.C. Krider & Bingham. 1821 pp.23ff.

[39] cf. Raymond M. Bost and Jeff L. Norris. *All One Body: The Story of The North Carolina Lutheran Synod 1803-1993.* Salisbury NC. Historical Committee, North Carolina Lutheran Synod. 1994 p. 347, note 47 and 49; and Socrates Henkel. *History of The Evangelical Lutheran Tennessee Synod.* p. 16. David's letter to Solomon is in the Special Collections at the University of Virginia Library, Charlottesville, VA. #8653-C, Box #1.

[40] This is certified by a number of members of David's Philadelphia congregation. The document is in the Handley Library, Miller Collection. Winchester, VA.

[41] ibid.

[42] The excommunication is authenticated in a deposition from several members

of the Philadelphia congregation dated October 16, 1819 located in the Handley Library, Miller Collection.
[43] This based on certification made by Adam Clonninger and Jacob Costner and held in the Handley Library, Miller Collection.
[44] This is based on notes made by David shortly after the meeting. They are found in the David Henkel Papers at Gettysburg Seminary, Gettysburg, PA.
[45] Shober to David Henkel, October 20, 1818. David Henkel papers. Gettysburg Lutheran Seminary.
[46] ibid. italics added.
[47] ibid.
[48] ibid.
[49] ibid.
[50] A copy of Andrew Hoyle's memorial to the North Carolina Synod is contained in the appendix to Gottlieb Shober's *Review of a Pamphlet ... by David Henkel*. 1821. North Carolina Synod Archives, Salisbury, NC. While the interpretation differs, the substance is essentially as described by David Henkel in his own description of his oath before Hoyle, Handley Library. Miller Collection; and his description of his trial, David Henkel Papers, Gettysburg Lutheran Seminary Library, Gettysburg, PA.
[51] Socrates Henkel. *History of the Evangelical Lutheran Tennessee Synod*. New Market, Virginia. The Henkel Press, 1890. pp.13f
[52] David Jay Webber. "Confessing the Faith in The language of America." *Logia*, vol IV, No. 3, July, 1995.
[53] Letter of Jacob Aderholt to WilliamVickers. April 16, 1818.
[54] cf. Carolinian Herald of Libery p. 41
[55] This is certified by David's ministerial colleague Daniel Moser in a certificate of October 9, 1819 contained in the Handley Library Miller Collection. It is repeated by David in *Carolinian Herald of Liberty*, p.41.
[56] ibid.
[57] cf. *Carolinian Herald of Liberty*, p.23f.
[58] Shober. *Review of a Pamphlet ...* p. 35
[59] ibid. pp.35-36
[60] The letters, dated May 31, 1819 and August 9, 1819 are found in the University of Virginia Special Collections 8653-C, Box #1.
[61] David Henkel. *Carolinian Herald of Liberty*. Salisbury, NC. Kreider & Kreider. 1821 pp. 25ff.
[62] ibid.
[63] *Carolinian Herald of Liberty*, pp. 31 -41
[64] ibid. p.46
[65] ibid.
[66] In the sixteenth century much such argument swirled around the Reformed Heidelberg Catechism of 1564 and its appendix on sacramental teaching, the so-called *Buchlein von Brotbrechen*.
[67] *Carolinian Herald of Liberty*, ibid.
[68] ibid.
[69] ibid.
[70] David Henkel. *Heavenly Flood of Regeneration*. Salisbury. Bingham & White,

Printers. 1822

[71] *Heavenly Flood of Regeneration*, p.6

[72] Helmuth was Pastor in Pennsylvania and several time President of the Ministerium of Pennsylvania.

[73] *Heavenly Flood of Regeneration*, p.7

[74] ibid.

[75] ibid.

[76] ibid.p.8

[77] ibid. p.9

[78] ibid. p.13

[79] ibid

[80] ibid p.13f.

[81] ibid. pp14-18

[82] ibid. 18-21

[83] ibid. p.22

[84] ibid. italics in the original

[85] ibid. p.28

[86] ibid.

[87] ibid. p.29

[88] ibid. p.30

[89] ibid. pp.30-31

[90] ibid. p33

[91] ibid. p.35

[92] ibid. pp.36-37

[93] ibid. pp.37-39

[94] ibid. p. 48

[95] ibid. p. 37

[96] ibid. p. 42

[97] ibid. p.43

[98] ibid. p.44

[99] ibid.

[100] ibid. pp45-46

[101] ibid. p.47

[102] ibid. p.48

[103] David Henkel. *Answer to Mr. Joseph Moore The Methodist with a few Fragments on the Doctrine of Justification*. New Market, Va. Printed in S. Henkel's Office, by S.G. Henkel. 1825

[104] Answer to Mr. Joseph Moore ... p.3 -4

[105] ibid. p.5 The words of the quote belong to Mr. Moore as quoted by David.

[106] ibid.

[107] ibid.

[108] ibid. p.6

[109] ibid. p.7

[110] ibid. p.8

[111] ibid. p.9

[112] ibid.

[113] ibid.pp.10-11

[114] ibid.
[115] ibid.
[116] ibid. p.16
[117] ibid. p.23
[118] ibid. p.24
[119] ibid.
[120] ibid.
[121] ibid. pp.24-25
[122] ibid. italics added.
[123] ibid. p.26
[124] ibid. pp.26-27
[125] ibid. pp.27-28
[126] ibid.
[127] ibid. p.29
[128] ibid. p.36
[129] ibid.
[130] ibid.
[131] ibid. p.37
[132] ibid.pp.38-39
[133] ibid.
[134] ibid. p.40
[135] ibid. p.41
[136] *David Henkel Against The Unitarians*. New Market. The Evangelical Lutheran Tennessee Synod. 1830.
[137] ibid. p.3
[138] ibid.pp.4-5
[139] ibid. p.6
[140] ibid.p.7
[141] ibid.p.8
[142] ibid.p.9-10
[143] It is to be noted that the Unitarians of Henkel's day were more akin to the Arians of the ancient church history than to modern Unitarians. However wrong they may have been, they intended to be biblical Christians and to appropriately honor Christ on the basis of the testimony of Holy Scripture, which the held to be authoritative in some way. Modern Unitarians could not be appealed to on the same basis since they have junked any notion of the Bible's authority over human religion.
[144] ibid.pp.10-16
[145] ibid. pp.21ff.
[146] ibid. pp. 27-31
[147] ibid. p. 34. David's citation is according to the King James text, although he seems to have a Greek New Testament in front of Him (see below). The Byzantine Majority text and the Textus Receptus, which form the textual basis of the KJV, both include the word *kurios*, which modern critical editions omit.
[148] ibid. p. 35
[149] ibid. p. 36
[150] ibid. p. 39
[151] ibid. p.40f.

[152] ibid. p. 48
[153] ibid. pp. 48-49
[154] ibid. pp. 49-50
[155] ibid.
[156] ibid. p. 52
[157] ibid. p. 53
[158] ibid. p. 54
[159] ibid. p. 56
[160] ibid. pp. 86ff.
[161] ibid. pp. 97-98
[162] The reference, not further specified is most likely the *Enchiridion cum Calvinistum* of the younger Lucas Osiander (1571—1638).
[163] His Translation of The Heidelberg Catechism is according to the Philadelphia edition of 1812.
[164] *David Henkel Against the Unitarians.* p.104
[165] ibid. pp.116-118
[166] ibid.

DAVID HENKEL

AGAINST THE UNITARIANS

A
TREATISE
ON
THE PERSON AND INCARNATION OF
JESUS CHRIST,
IN WHICH SOME OF THE PRINCIPAL
ARGUMENTS OF THE
UNITARIANS ARE
EXAMINED.

PUBLISHED BY ORDER OF THE EVANGELICAL
LUTHERAN TENNESSEE SYNOD.

NEW-MARKET:
PRINTED IN S. HENKEL'S OFFICE.

1830

EASTERN DISTRICT OF VIRGINIA, to wit:

BE IT REMEMBERED, That on the fourth day of January in the fifty fourth year of the independence of the United States of America, Solomon Henkel, of the said district, hath deposited in this office, the title of a book, the right whereof he claims as proprietor, in the words following, to wit:

"David Henkel against the Unitarians. A treatise on the person and incarnation of Jesus Christ, in which some of the principal arguments of the Unitarians are examined. Published by order of the Evangelical Lutheran Tennessee Synod."

In conformity to the act of the Congress of the United States, entitled "an act for the encouragement of learning, by securing the copies of maps, charts, and books, to the authors and proprietors of such copies, during the times therein mentioned."

R. JEFFRIES,
Clerk of the Eastern District of Virginia

SECTION I.

One of the principal arguments of the Unitarians is, that there can be no difference shewn between three divine persons and three beings. This is examined, and the distinction between the Father and the Son is somewhat elucidated.

That God is but one being is admitted by all Christian denominations, and also by Mahometans, Deists and Devils. I shall therefore offer no proof in behalf of his unity. But that three persons are God deserves an investigation to ascertain whether or not such an idea is repugnant to his unity. Since God is but one being, Unitarians conclude that he is also only one in person: for they do not seem to perceive the least difference between a divine being and person. Accordingly, they employ this as one of their principal positions, from thence deducing sundry apparent formidable objections against the doctrine of Christ's eternal Godhead. For if no difference can be shewn between a divine being and person, then consequently, as the Father is God, Christ cannot also be God, without admitting a plurality of supreme Gods.

The Rev. James Miller in a pamphlet entitled *Trinitarianism Unmasked* says: "I defy Trinitarians to make a plain and scriptural distinction between a self-existent and intelligent substance, and a self-existent and intelligent subsistence; or to prove that it takes three self-existent and intelligent subsistences to make one substance." p. 37. Again, "But notwithstanding the variety of opinions which have been formed on the subject, I shall endeavor to maintain the position that intelligent person, and intelligent being, are the same, or terms of synonymous signification; etc." p. 43. He then proceeds, endeavoring to shew from sundry texts of Scripture that human beings and persons are terms of a synonymous signification. It must be admitted that the term *person* generally denotes an intelligent being, having [his] own separate existence, not subsisting in another. This term is also used with respect to God. Notwithstanding it would be incorrect to infer that the term *person* relative to God indicated the very same in all respects as when applied to men and angels. Indeed, the Scriptures employ terms relative to God and heavenly things, answering to things in nature. Without such terms, the Scriptures would be utterly unintelligible. Notwithstanding this analogous language, it does not follow that heavenly and divine things in their substance, and in all their relations are precisely like things in nature. As for instance: God is called a Father, which is a term corresponding to a relation among men, i.e. to a human father; yet it is evident that he in many respects is not like a human father. For all human fathers have a beginning of their existence, they are changeful and mortal; whereas God is very different in these respects, for he is self-existent, eternal, immutable and immortal.

If the term *person* relative to God implied the same in all respects as when applied to man, then the term being would imply the same in either case.

Mr. Miller taking for granted that a human person implies the same as a divine person, he presumes that the idea of three persons being God is highly absurd. For he says: "Can any person believe that three human persons make but one man? How then can any man of common sense believe that three divine persons, each possessed of infinite perfections, make but one God?" p. 93. Thus comparing God to a man, the same as Mr. Miller compares human to divine persons, he might also easily prove away all his supreme perfections. For if, as Mr. M. says: person and being are the same, and if the absurdity of three persons be inferred from the impossibility of three human persons being one man, then upon the same principle, it might be concluded that God is neither self-existent, nor eternal, nor omnipotent, nor infinite. Why so? Answer. Because according to Mr. M's logic, it might be said: can any person believe that a human person in self-existent, eternal, omnipotent and infinite? How then can any man of common sense believe that God is self-existent, eternal, omnipotent and infinite? Such a conclusion is groundless. Nevertheless, Mr. M. has introduced such, to overthrow the doctrine of the Trinity: viz. because three human persons are not one man, therefore three divine persons cannot be one God. Is it congenial to correct logic to conclude that the mode of God's existence is like that of man? Is it not an invariable rule in sound reasoning never to admit any thing in the conclusion which cannot be deduced from the premises? As for instance: how absurd it would be, if one introduced a subject relative to an angel, and then brought out his conclusion upon a reptile! A correct reasoner never concludes any thing which is not susceptible of being deduced from the premises. In reasoning on the being and relations of God, it would be absurd to confound him with any thing that is created, or to illustrate his character in this manner: unless he himself has indicated the clue in the Scriptures. If any person would properly prove the doctrine of the Trinity absurd, he ought by no means to conclude that three divine persons are not one God, because three men are not one man: for thus God and created things would be confounded, which would be incorrect, in as much as not every thing deducible from created things, is also deducible from divine things, since there is a great difference between that which is created, and that which is uncreated. Let such as consider this doctrine absurd prove it, if they be able, by shewing it to be repugnant to God's essence, character, attributes and relations; and thus constitute their premises of divine things, then their conclusion may be correct.

I should by no means venture to illustrate the distinction between the Father's and Christ's persons by any comparison in nature, unless such be clearly indicated by the Scriptures. In distinguishing Christ from the Father, I shall briefly view the following text: "Who being the brightness of his glory, and the express image of his person." Heb. 1:3.

If Christ be the brightness of the Father's glory, then the Father himself must be a light: for a brightness presupposes a light. God in the Scriptures is called a light, a fire, a sun, as for instance: "God is light," 1 John 1:5. comp. Isa. 60:19, 20; "the Lord thy God is a consuming fire," Deut. 4:24—comp. ch 9:3, Heb. 12:29; "For the Lord God is a sun and shield." Ps. 84:11. As the nature of the light is, so is also the nature of its brightness.

A created light reflects a created brightness, but an uncreated light reflects an uncreated brightness. God is an eternal, uncreated light, Christ is the brightness of his glory; consequently Christ is eternal and uncreated. The brightness of a light is also truly light, yet distinguished from the light by which it is reflected. Or properly, the brightness of the luminary is the luminary itself reflected. Christ is the brightness of God's glory, God is a light, a sun, hence Christ is God reflected. As God is a light, even so Christ is a light; hence not such a light as John the Baptist, who was a burning and shining light. John 5:35. John is called ο λυχνος, which signifies a lamp, or a candle made of wax or tallow; hence no original light, whereas Christ is called Το φως αληθινον, the true light. Indeed, he cannot be otherwise than the true eternal light, for he is the brightness of the glory of God, who is the true uncreated light. The brightness may not be distinguished from its luminary: for the brightness does not reflect the luminary, but the brightness is reflected by the luminary. Christ being the brightness of God's glory, he is distinguished from God, inasmuch as God is not reflected, or begotten by him, but he is reflected, or begotten by the Father. Although, the brightness may be distinguished from its luminary; yet it is not another luminary, and it cannot be properly said, that because the luminary and brightness may be distinguished, they are two luminaries. Neither is the brightness merely one of the qualities, nor only a part of the luminary: for the luminary with its plenitude is indivisibly reflected in the brightness. Christ is the brightness of God's glory, but he is not merely one of his attributes, nor only a part of the Father: for he is God himself reflected; all the divine fulness is in this resplendence; therefore Christ is the Father's substance in the reflection, and as little as the luminary and its brightness constitute two luminaries, even so little the Father and Christ are two Gods, or beings. If, as the Unitarians suppose, Christ were a distinct being from God, how then could he be the brightness of his glory? To suppose Christ to be a distinct being from God, would also suppose this text to be false, because the brightness of no luminary is a separate luminary from the one from which it proceeds. Now Unitarians, in asserting that Christ is a distinct being from the Father, are in a dilemma: for as much as they must either suppose that a brightness can be separated in such a manner from its luminary so as to constitute a distinct substance; or they must utterly deny that Christ is the brightness of God's glory. To suppose the former would be contrary to fact: for no brightness can be separated from its luminary, not even for a moment, because the brightness always perpetually adheres to, and flows from, its luminary; and to deny that Christ is the brightness of God's glory would be roundly denying the declaration of God's word. Whatever objections Unitarians may allege, they shall never be able to overthrow this invincible truth: that Christ is the brightness of God's glory; consequently, though distinct as a brightness, yet the same God.

Christ is not only said to be the brightness of God, but the brightness of his glory. His glory must be his chief excellence, an uncreated prerogative above all creatures; or his supreme perfections. The prophet saith: "I am the Lord: that is my name: and my glory will I not give to another, neither my praise to graven images." Isa. 42:8. The glory of God according to this text is something which is not at all to be communicated to any other being, for it declares:"my glory will I not give to another"; hence is his exclusive prerogative and characteristic. The Psalmist says: "the heavens declare the glory of God, and the firmament sheweth his handy work." Ps. 19:1. The heavens, in declaring his glory, manifest his supreme perfections: such as omnipotence, wisdom, etc. St. Paul also says: "the invisible things from the creation of the world are clearly seen, being understood by the things that are made, even his eternal power and Godhead." Rom. 1:20. To see the eternal power and Godhead by the creation is the same as the heavens declaring his glory. Thus God's glory is his supreme perfections, of which he declares that he will not give to another, and which exalt him in the sight of intelligent creatures as the only object of adoration. What then is the brightness of his glory? Answer. All the supreme perfections of God in the reflection. But can this reflection, or brightness, constitute a separate and distinct being from God? By no means. For if so, God's glory, which he declares that he will not give to another, would be the glory of another being, i.e. Christ, who is the brightness of his glory. The brightness of God's glory, is the self-same glory reflected. Now since God declares that he will not give his glory to another, and yet as Christ is this glory in the reflection, it is evident, that he is by no means a separate being from his Father, though different in so far as he is reflected.

Christ is not only the brightness of God's glory, but also the "express image of his person." The word χαραχτηρ, rendered by the translators *express image*, properly signifies an impression by a stamp or type. It also signifies the impression on coins of gold and silver, and engravings in stones, wood and metals. Not every image is an express image, for some images are mere painted resemblances of things and persons; but χαραχτηρ implies much more, it being an impression of a stamp. The word υποστασις, rendered *person*, from υφιστημι, *to place under*, properly denotes a reality, substance, or existence. Christ is the impression of God's substance or existence. Now if the very substance of a stamp were impressed, would not also the nature and all the qualities of which it consisted, be conspicuously and substantially in the impression? Christ is the impression of God's substance; hence God's own substance, or existence, is perpetually, essentially, absolutely and indelibly impressed in him; so that the Father is in, and identified with, his person; for he saith: "he that hath seen me, hath seen the Father." Joh. 44:9.

The difference between a stamp and its impression is easily perceived. Christ is an impression, which has the Father's substance: for he is the express image of his person; consequently he is the same substance of the Father, and yet he is distinct from him; because the Father is impressed in him, but he is not impressed in the Father. Now since Christ is the impression of God's substance, how then can he be a separate being? If he were a separate substance, he could not be an impression of God's substance.

IMPROVEMENT

It has been shewn that God is a light, he is not a created, but a self-existent light. No light exists without a resplendence: for it is peculiar to every light to reflect itself. Where is there any light, which ever existed one moment prior to its brightness? Is God an uncreated self-existent light? Then surely he never existed without reflecting himself; or he never was without an uncreated self-existent brightness. It is by an absolute necessity that God reflects himself, because he is a light, and no light can exist without a brightness. God, the eternal light, did therefore never exist one moment prior to his brightness. Christ is the brightness of his glory; he therefore never existed prior to Christ, and according to his own nature, he could never have existed without him: for he is a light, and no light can exist without a brightness. God does not exist by the will of another being, but he exists necessarily, absolutely and independently; whereas every other being owes its existence to the will of the creator. But does Christ, like another being, owe his existence to the will of a creator? He that owes his existence to another one, might have been left in non-existence. Now does the brightness merely exist by the will of the light, so that it might have been left in non-existence? By no means: seeing that the brightness could as little have been left in non-existence as the light itself, and if it were possible to extinguish the brightness, the light itself would be extinguished. God exists absolutely and independently, and it is utterly impossible for him not to exist; he is a light, Christ is the brightness thereof. Hence as little as God could be in non-existence, so little Christ could be in non-existence; and if it were possible to annihilate Christ, it could not be done without annihilating the Father; because God is a light, and no light can possibly exist without a brightness; hence this brightness exists as absolutely and independently as the light itself. Now if it be asked: is not Christ dependent on God for his existence? I answer: if the brightness depend upon the light, then is Christ also dependent on God. The light itself is independent, and the brightness is the light itself reflected. God is an eternal, self-existent, independent light, and what is the brightness of such a light but the same eternal, self-existent light reflected? Christ is this brightness. He is, therefore, eternal and independent; nevertheless he by no means possesses a separate self-existence and independency, but the Father's self-same self-existence and independency.

SECTION II

Unitarians suppose that the Father is God alone to the exclusion of Christ, because the terms God and Father are synonymous, etc. This is examined, and it is more particularly shewn that the Father and Christ are one being.

  Mr. J. Miller supposes that because the Father only is called the supreme God, and that in the Scriptures the terms Father and God are used synonymously, that Christ is not God. He says, p. 80: "That the Father of Christ is alone the supreme God, will, it is believed, appear,

1. From the peculiar titles which the Scriptures ascribe to him, and the discriminating representations which they make concerning him." He quoted the following texts: Luke 1:32. Ps. 91:9. Gen. 14:18. Deut. 33:27. Matth. 16:16. Col. 1:15. John 17:3. Rom. 16:27. Rev. 19:6. James 1:17.

"That all," continues Mr. M., p. 81,"these passages relate to the Father of Christ, is too obvious, I should think, to admit of reasonable doubt, and that they confirm and establish the doctrine that he alone is the supreme God, appears equally obvious." Mr. M. then proceeds to put questions relative to these passages. He asks p. 81: "If the Father of Christ is the highest, the most high, the most high God, can any other person or being be as high. Surely no person or being can be so high as that person or being who is the most high." Again. "If the Father of Christ is the eternal God, can any other person or being have a just claim to the same title? Or can any person or being besides the Father, be considered the Eternal God? etc. If the Father of Christ is the living God, can we reasonably admit that any other person or being is also the living God? This cannot be admitted, unless we admit the idea of another God, distinct from the Father. If the Father of Christ is the invisible God whom no man hath seen nor can see, can this character be ascribed to any other person or being? Can it with truth be ascribed (p. 82.) to Christ, who was seen and handled by men, as well after his resurrection, as before his death? If the Father of Christ is the only true God, can there be another true God, or can the true God exist distinct from the Father; whom Christ calls the only true God? If glory is to be given to the Father as the only wise God, through Jesus Christ, can any other being have a just claim to the same glory through him? Or is it to be admitted, that although there is but one person only, who is independently and supremely wise. If the Father of Christ is the Lord God omnipotent, and who also reigneth by his own independent power, can there be any other person who is also the Lord God omnipotent, and who reigneth by his own independent power? If the Father of Christ is without variableness or shadow of turning, can it with truth be said of any other person, that he is also without variableness or shadow of turning? Even Jesus Christ, the Son and image of the Father, descended from riches to poverty, was literally subject to sorrow, grief, joy and gladness, and was like unto his brethren in temptations, sufferings, pain and death. From these considerations, are we not constrained to conclude that the Father of Christ is alone the supreme God?"

ANSWER. It is readily admitted that no other being beside the Father can be the eternal God, neither do Trinitarians believe that there is another supreme being, nor is this the point in question. But the controversy is whether, or not, the Father and Christ are one being. In the preceeding section I have proven by the text in Heb. 1:3 that he and the Father are one being; and yet, have shewn wherein they are distinguished. Although, the Father alone is the Eternal and living God; yet since Christ is one with him he is necessarily included in the same oneness. Suppose I affirmed that the sun was the only luminary of day to the exclusion of all others, and then concluded, that hence the brightness thereof could not be light, should I not be exploded? Nevertheless, Mr. M's inferences are similar: for he supposes that since he has proven that the Father alone is the eternal, living, true, omnipotent and independent God, that therefore, Christ is not the true God. Is not Christ the brightness of God's glory? If so, is he not one being with the Father? Since it has been shewn that Christ is the Father's substance reflected, this position is already sufficient to answer all such objections of the Unitarians, founded on texts, indicating supreme prerogatives, exclusively ascribed to the Father: viz. such as, the Father alone is the eternal, living, immutable, etc. God, who only hath immortality: for whatever glory or prerogative is ascribed to the Father, also belongs to the self-same uncreated light reflected in the person of Christ, who being the brightness of his glory; and it is by no means necessary that the same prerogatives in all the texts ascribed to the Father, should also particularly, be ascribed to Christ; because it is readily understood, that when the Father is named, the Son is also included in his unity; even as when we ascribe some quality to the sun, no man ever thinks that the brightness thereof is excluded, but is naturally supposed to be the sun itself reflected.

That Christ is one with the Father shews the propriety of calling him in sundry texts the only true God, which does not exclude Christ from being the same; and which also readily accounts for the propriety of the Scripture phrases addressing God in the singular number. Christ also differently from his son-ship, sustains another relation to the Father: for in the fulness of time he was made flesh, and thus was constituted a mediator. The Father is not the mediator; consequently Christ in so far as he is a mediator, is distinct from the Father; hence the Father alone in this respect is the only true God. This is according to 1 Tim. 1:5: "*there* is one God, and one mediator between God and men, the man Christ Jesus."

The passage in John 17:3—"this is life eternal, that they might know thee the only true God, and Jesus Christ, whom thou has sent;"—urged by Mr. M. does not exclude Christ from being one with the Father, but distinguishes him as one that was sent and a mediator. It must also be observed, that to know God is eternal life; now the very same is ascribed to the knowing of Christ. None but God can give eternal life, and none can receive it, but such as know him. Christ also gives eternal life, and by knowing him, we receive it; hence he and the Father are one being.

That the Father is the invisible God, and that Christ was visible, that is, seen and handled by men, does not prove that he and the Father are not one being. It ought to be remembered that in the fullness of time the Son was made flesh. But how could he have been made flesh and be crucified, without also becoming visible? Mr. M. and, as far as I know, all Unitarians believe that the Holy Ghost is one thing with the Father: for they do not even admit that he is a distinct person. Now I ask, was the Holy Ghost never visible? Did he not appear in a bodily shape like a dove, descending on our Saviour at his baptism in Jordan? Now if this be urged as a reason that Christ is not God—because he was visible after had assumed a human body—then upon the same ground it might also be urged that the Holy Ghost cannot be God's Spirit: because God is invisible, whereas the Holy Ghost was seen in a bodily shape. Mr. M. concludes: the Father is invisible; Christ was seen; therefore they are two distinct beings. What would he reply, if I also concluded: the Father is invisible; the Holy Ghost was seen in the visible shape of a dove; therefore the Holy Ghost is a distinct being from the Father? Would he, or any other Unitarian, admit that God's Spirit is a distinct being from himself? By no means: for they teach the contrary doctrine.

I Cor. 8:6: "But to us there is but one God, the Father, of whom are all things." On this Mr. M. observes, p. 85: "If the Father, of whom are all things, is the one God, can it be true that the one God consists of two persons besides the Father?"

ANSWER. The apostle also in the same verse adds: "and one Lord Jesus Christ, by whom are all things, and we by him." Why is it said: "but to us there is but one God, the Father"? In opposition to the many Gods of the heathens as the context shews, viz. "As concerning therefore the eating of those things that are offered in sacrifice unto idols, we know that an idol is nothing in the world, and that there is none other God but one, for though there be [those] that are called Gods, whether in heaven or in earth, (as there be Gods many, and Lords many,)" v. 4, 5. Thus it is evident that the Father is God alone in opposition to the many Gods of the heathens. Or does the apostle rank Christ with the many Gods and Lords? If the Father alone exclusively of Christ is God, then it is evident that Christ is one of the idols, who are excluded from being God: for the apostle shews that the Father is the true God in opposition to the many Gods and Lords so called. Christ is not one of the many Gods and Lords whom the apostle opposes to the one God, for he does not only say: "but to us there is but one God, the Father, of whom are all things," but adds: "and one Lord Jesus Christ, by whom are all things, and we by him." Thus if Christ is the one Lord, how can he be one of the many Gods and Lords? Mr. M. has attempted to prove that the Father exclusively of Christ is God, because the text says: "but to us there is but one God, the Father." Now if the Father exclusively of Christ is God, then Christ also exclusively of the Father is Lord: for as emphatically as the text declares, that the Father only, is God; even so emphatically also, it declares that Christ only is Lord: "and one Lord Jesus Christ." Let me ask Mr. M. or any other Unitarian: whether the Father is Lord? Would they deny that he is Lord? I presume not. But how is it possible for the Father to be Lord, when Christ is the one Lord? Christ being the one Lord, can the Father also be the Lord without supposing two Lords? Will Unitarians affirm that there are two Lords? If they do, they would contradict the apostle, who says that Christ is Lord; and if they deny that the Father is Lord, they would contradict Moses, who says: "Hear, O

Israel; the Lord our God is one Lord." Deut. 6:4. Thus God is called one Lord, but how can he be the Lord, when St. Paul says Christ is the Lord, without contradicting either Paul or Moses? Now how can Unitarians reconcile this: that Christ is the one Lord, and yet, that the Father also is the Lord, without supposing two Lords? I do not understand how to reconcile this, without admitting that the Father is called the one God, and Christ the one Lord in opposition to the many idols of the heathens: but neither is God one in opposition to Christ, nor Christ one Lord in opposition to the Father. Again, if the Father and Christ are one being, then either may be called the one Lord without excluding the other.

Mr. M. Says, p. 83: "When John said, 'who shall not fear thee, O Lord, and glorify thy name, for thou only art holy?' are we to understand that he had exclusive reference to the Lord Jesus Christ? Is it not more reasonable to infer that he had particular reference to the most high God, his Father? That this inference is correct, the preceding verse furnishes, I think, conclusive evidence. 'And they sing the song of Moses, the servant of God, and the song of the Lamb, saying great and marvelous are thy works, Lord God Almighty, just and true are thy ways, thou King of saints.' Here the person alluded to, in the text under consideration, is expressly called the Lord God Almighty; and who is the Lord God Almighty but the Father of Christ? He is none other; therefore the Father of Christ is the only independently holy being, and the fountain of holiness to his creatures."

ANSWER. It seems that Mr. M. concludes, that because the Father is said to be only holy [that is, the only holy one], therefore Christ is not Almighty God. Now if supreme holiness (which is most certainly true) is a proof of an eternal Godhead, then surely Christ is God. Christ is holy: "thou wilt not leave my soul in hell, neither wilt thou suffer thine holy One to see corruption." Acts 2:27. Christ is not only the holy One, but he is positively the most holy. "Seventy weeks are determined upon thy people, and upon thy holy city, to finish the transgression, and to make an end of sins, and to make reconciliation for iniquity, and to bring in everlasting righteousness, and to seal up the vision and prophecy, and to anoint THE MOST HOLY." Dan. 9:24.

Who is the person anointed? Surely not the Father? For he never was anointed. The passage speaks of the Messiah. See also v. 25, 26. The word Christ signifies one that is anointed. Thus it is evident that Jesus is the person alluded to in the text, he is positively called the most holy; the most holy was anointed; hence Christ is the most holy. See also Heb. 2. Now according to Mr. Miller's logic, can any one be as holy as the most holy? If the Father only is holy, how can Christ be the most holy? It is in vain to urge that holiness was communicated to Christ in a greater measure than to other men, that therefore he is called the most holy: for if he had not an original independent holiness, he could not be the most holy, as his Father only would be the most holy. Now if Christ and the Father were not consubstantial, would it be possible to shew how the Father only is holy; and yet that Christ also is the most holy? This could not upon any other ground be reconciled. But when it is shewn that the Father and the Son are consubstantial, it may easily be understood. Now Mr. M. must admit either that the Father was anointed, or that the Son is the most holy. That the Father was anointed cannot be proven: for had he ever been anointed there would be two Christs. Again, if Christ, as the Unitarians suppose, be a distinct essence, hence a distinct being from the Father, then it would follow that Christ would be far superior to the Father in holiness, because Christ is the most holy. Two different substances cannot both be the most holy. But Christ is positively said to be the most holy; and yet who can deny that the Father is the most holy? When both are most holy, it must be concluded that they are one substance.

Mr. M. observes p. 83 and 84: "When Paul said, 'who only hath immortality, etc.' is it not undeniably evident that he had exclusive reference to the invisible God, the Father of Christ? This is not only evident from the 16th verse, which has been already adduced, but also from the preceding verses." Again, "If, then, the Father of Christ, the one God, the invisible Jehovah, whom no man hath seen nor can see, if he and he alone possesses goodness, holiness and immortality, in an absolute, infinite, eternal, independent and supreme sense, and is therefore the fountain and source of goodness, holiness and immortality, to all rational and intelligent existence, can any other person or being be the possessor of those attributes in the same sense? Can they with truth or propriety be ascribed, in the same sense, to Christ, who was the first begotten of the Father, who lives by him, who received all things from him, and who became obedient unto death, even the death of the cross? Surely they cannot. Therefore the most high, invisible God, the Father of Christ, is alone the supreme God."

ANSWER. I shall by no means deny that this text has a reference to the Father. Nevertheless, Christ is not excluded from having immortality. He says, "I am the way, and the truth, and the life." John 14:6. Truly, a being may live without possessing absolute immortality: for it may be sustained by another source of life; but that any one should be life itself, as Christ is said to be, without having immortality, is out of the question. Again, "For as the Father hath life in himself, so hath he given to the Son to have life in himself." John 5:26. What is the Father's life in himself? It is an absolute, underived immortality. No creature has life in itself: for all creatures have derived their lives from, and live and move in God; but his life cannot possibly flow from another fountain: for it is self-original. Now it is positively said, as the Father has life in himself, so hath he given to the Son to have life in himself; hence the Son has positively the Father's self-original life in himself. Christ's life is not different from the Father's: for the self-immortal Father is the light of his own brightness, i.e. Christ; therefore he possesses the same self-existent life. Now as absolute immortality is a prerogative of God, it is evident that Christ is God, because he is life, and because the Father gave him to have life in himself; even as he has it in himself.

That the Father is only wise, Rom. 16:27, does not prove that Christ is not God. Is not Christ the wisdom of God? Is it not so said in Prov. 8, and 1 Cor. 1:24? Christ is wisdom—yea, the wisdom of God—and yet not one being with the Father! How strange! God only is wise, Christ is the wisdom of God; hence if they are not one being, then God has two wisdoms! But who can believe this?

IMPROVEMENT

The more clearly it can be shewn that the Father and Christ are one being, the more evidently it will appear that Christ is God. Christ said unto Philip: "Believest thou not, that I *am* in the Father, and the Father in me? The words that I speak unto you, I speak not of myself: but the Father that dwelleth in me, he doeth the works. Believe me that I am in the Father, and the Father in me: or else believe me for the very work's sake." John 14:10, 11. Thus since the Father is in the Son, and the Son in the Father, and the Father doeth the works in him, the one does not exist nor act without the other. Two separate beings also exist separately: for how otherwise could I know two distinct beings, unless they also existed distinctly? Although the Son be personally distinct from the Father, yet he (as this text shews) exists in the Father. Where do we see a human son exist in his father and his father in him? But if such a sight were possible, it could not otherwise be concluded than that they were one being. No human son is in his father, and his father in him, but they exist separately; hence are two distinct beings. But Christ is never out of his Father, nor the Father out of him; hence no separate existence of either is perceivable; therefore they are one being.

But lest it should be objected that God also dwells in saints, and they in him, I shall observe that the Scriptures no where represent the union of saints with God in the same relation as that of the Father and the Son. The context indicates by Christ being in the Father and he in him a different relation than that of saints to God. Philip desired to see the Father, saying: "Lord shew us the Father, and it sufficeth us. Jesus saith unto him, have I been so long time with you, and yet hast thou not known me, Philip? He that hath seen me, hath seen the Father; and how sayest thou then, shew us the Father?" v. 8, 9. Why would Christ have told Philip, that whosoever saw him also saw the Father, if he intended to indicate nothing more than that the Father simply dwells in him like in the saints? For according to this, in seeing any saint, one would see the Father. This would be absurd: for is it possible to suppose that because God dwells in the saints he is identified with their persons, so that upon seeing any of them one would see God? No! Now it must be concluded that when Christ is said to be in the Father and he in him, and that when in consequence of this, upon seeing Christ the Father is seen, that they both are identified, i. e. they are one being. If Christ and the Father were two distinct beings, then by all means Christ could have been seen separately from the Father: for two distinct beings may also be discerned distinctly and separately. But Christ is not seen without the Father, therefore Christ and the Father are one being.

This passage seems to be parallel with that recorded in Exod. 23:20, 21: The Lord says, "Behold, I send an angel before thee, to keep thee in the way, and to bring thee into the place which I have prepared. Beware of him, and obey his voice, provoke him not; for he will not pardon your transgressions: for my name is in him." This angel seems to have a divine prerogative; seeing that he has the power to pardon or not to pardon transgressions, and Jehovah's name is in him. The name JEHOVAH is the proper name of the supreme Being, and it can easily be shewn that it is indicative of his perfections. This name is in the angel that was sent. But the angel was distinct in personality from the one that sent him; yet as Jehovah's name was in him, and that name is indicative of supreme perfections, it seems this angel had supreme perfections: hence one being with Jehovah. If this angel was not Christ, I am utterly at a loss to know any rational interpretation on the text.

The prophet says: "I am the Lord: that is my name; and my glory will I not give to another, neither my praise to graven images." Isa. 42:8. Now if it be proven that God gave his glory to Christ, then it follows either that Christ is not another being, or else that the prophet asserted a falsehood in declaring that God would not give his glory to another. It has already been shewn that this glory is all the supreme perfections of God, and that Christ is the brightness thereof; hence the same glory reflected. Unitarians themselves acknowledge that supreme perfections are communicated to Christ. Mr. Worcester says: that Christ is almighty by the indwelling of the Father, or the fullness of the Godhead, and that it is possible for persons to receive divine perfections, etc. See *Bible News*, p. 75, 76. Mr. Miller also acknowledges that the fullness of God dwells in Christ. Now if according to the concessions of Unitarians, Christ be almighty by the indwelling of the Father, and is possessed of divine fullness, then by all means he has the Father's glory. Christ says: "and now, O Father, glorify thou me with thine own self, with the glory which I had with thee before the world was." John 17:5. With what glory did Christ pray to be glorified? Answer. With the Father himself, for he says: "glorify thou me with thine own self"; and he also declares that he had this same glory before the world was. He that is glorified with the Father himself, and who had this glory before the creation of the world, possesses the uncreated, supreme glory. Since Christ has this glory—and yet, as the prophet declares, that God will not give his glory to another—it undeniably follows that God and his Son are one and the same being.

SECTION III

Christ is the only begotten Son of God. It is shewn that although some attempt to prove because he is a son, his Father is anterior to him; nevertheless his sonship proves his eternal Deity.

That Christ is the only begotten Son of God is evident from sundry passages of the Scripture; neither is this position denied by Unitarians, nor by any other Christian denomination with whom I am acquainted. Nevertheless, because he is the Son of God, Unitarians conclude that he is not God. Mr. James Miller says, "The term Father implies that the Lord Jesus Christ is a son; but if the relative terms, Father and Son, do not denote two real intelligent persons or beings, by what words or language can such a distinction be denoted? Do not the terms *father* and *son* necessarily denote anteriority of existence in the person of the Father and posteriority of existence in the person of the Son, and that the Son derived his existence and nature from the Father? Must not these terms then, in relation to the supreme God and his only begotten Son, be strangely perverted if we so construe them as to make them signify one and the same being—that the Son is really the Father, and that the Father is really the Son; or that the Father and Son are one numerical being, or God? Does not such a construction of these relative terms seem, in the highest degree unnatural?" p. 87.

Mr. Worcester says, "So far as the natural import of language is to be regarded, the terms, a *self-existent son*, imply a real and palpable contradiction. The term *self-existent* is perfectly opposed to the term son, and the term *son* is perfectly opposed to *self-existence*. If there be any term in our language which naturally implies *derived existence*, the term *son* is of this import. To affirm that a person is a *derived self-existent Being* implies no greater contradiction than to affirm that a person is a *self-existent son*. And to affirm that Jesus Christ is personally the self-existent God, and at the same time *truly* the SON of God, is precisely the same contradiction that it would be to affirm that the *Prince of Wales* is truly *King George the Third*, and also truly the SON of King George the Third." *Bible News*, page 55, 56.

Positions like these to disprove the consubstantiality of Christ with the Father are not only urged by Unitarians, but also by some who profess Christ as God, seeing they deny that he is God's Son according to his divine nature. They predicate his sonship merely upon his miraculous conception, and his birth of the virgin Mary.

Mr. Isaac Lewis in a treatise against Mr. J. Miller, attempts to prove that Christ is the Son of God according to his humanity only, and denies the sonship of his divinity. He says, p. 7, "I say he is the Son of God in reference to his miraculous conception." In this he has followed Mr. Adam Clarke.

That the existence of a father is prior to that of a son, is true with respect to men, for they are created beings. The begetting of a son also takes place in time, and who after his birth has a separate and distinct existence of his father. Such as deny the sonship of Christ's divinity upon the supposition that the father must exist prior to the son, compare God and his son to a man and his son, and confound human with divine generation. To compare the generation of God's Son with that of a man's son is absurd. For if there be the least propriety in it, the existence of God might also be compared with that of a man. But who would suppose that God's existence is like that of a man? I presume, no one. Now if God is not like a man, with what propriety can the generation of his Son be compared with human generation? Every human father descended from a father himself, and even the first man having been created had a beginning. A being begets its like—a human father having descended from a father cannot beget a son, who has not also a beginning. God the Father neither had a beginning, nor a father prior to himself. How then can any one conclude that his Son is like the sons of men, or that he like they must be posterior to his Father? Such a conclusion is absurd, seeing God bears no analogy to human fathers.

That the relative terms *father* and *son* denote two distinct beings, and anteriority and posteriority of existence is indeed true with respect to men, but how do Unitarians or others prove that it implies the same when applied to God and his Son? If God were like a man, they might establish this hypothesis. But since he is not like a man, it is vain to compare the generation of God's Son with that of the son of a man, or to suppose that the relative terms *father* and *son* when applied to God and his Son denote two distinct beings or anteriority and posteriority of existence.

How do Unitarians prove that the term *a self-existent son* implies a real and palpable contradiction, and that the term *self-existent* is perfectly opposed to the term *son*, and the term *son* to *self-existent?* They cannot, unless it were correct to compare God and his Son to a man and his son. Such a supposition is repugnant to the rules of logic. Nevertheless, if it were possible to suppose such to be correct, it would also prove that God the Father is not self-existent: for a human father is as little self-existent as a son.

In reasoning correctly it will appear that every being begets its like. Man begets man. A man's son is as really and substantially a man as his father, possessing his nature! As a human father is a dependent creature, existing in time; even so his son is dependent, having a beginning. Now if God begat a son, why should he not also be like God, possessing his very nature? Is it possible for God to have an only begotten Son, without having his nature and attributes? To suppose Christ to be God's only begotten Son without admitting him to possess Jehovah's nature and perfections, is indeed a palpable contradiction. Viewed in this light Christ would be a son without his father's nature. How strange to suppose a son without possessing his father's nature. Is not self-existence peculiar to God? Are not the perfections of eternity, infinity, immutability, etc. essential to his character? Now how is it possible for God to have a son, who is destitute of his nature and perfections? If God was like a man, his son would also be like the son of a man. But since God is self-existent, eternal, immutable, etc. it must follow that his only begotten Son is like himself: viz. the impression of his substance.

Mr. Worcester says, "That God is a self-existent Being, is acknowledged by all Christians; and I shall freely admit, that it is *impossible* with God to beget or produce a *self-existent* son." p. 72, 73.

How does Mr. Worcester know that this is impossible with God? By what passage of Scripture does he prove this impossibility? By none. Are not all things possible with God? If so, upon what authority can any man affirm that it is impossible with God to beget a self-existent son? He says, page 58, "We also find, that God has endued the various tribes of creatures with a power of procreation, by which they produce offspring in their own likeness. Why is it not as possible that God should possess the power of producing a SON in his own likeness, or with his own nature, as that he should be able to endue his creatures with such a power?" This is by all means an accurate observation. Nevertheless, Mr. W. himself argues very repugnant to this his own position, when he most confidently asserts that it is impossible with God to beget, or produce a self-existent son. If every tribe of creatures be endued with the power of procreation, by which they produce offspring in their own likeness, upon what ground can Mr. W. deny that it is impossible with God to beget a self-existent son, when self-existence is a peculiar characteristic of his being? To evade the force of this argument, Mr. W. observes, "It may not be necessary that every attribute of Deity should be communicable or derivable in order that he may have an OWN SON among the children of men, it is not necessary to the existence or the idea of a *son*, that he should possess *all* the attributes, properties, or qualities of his father. Nor is it necessary that he should possess *no other* attributes but such as were possessed by his father. Among the seventy sons of Gideon, perhaps, there were no two that perfectly resembled each other in their attributes, properties or qualities; and probably no one who was the perfect likeness of his father. So Jesus Christ may have truly derived his existence and nature from God, and yet not possess every attribute of the Father." p. 74.

This argument is not correct in every respect. Truly not all the children of men are exactly like their fathers in every respect. They also derive certain qualities from their mothers and some they acquire by habit and education. Although no man's son may in all respects be like his father; yet he certainly possesses the same human nature, and the qualities peculiar to men. Where is the son of any man who does not possess man's nature? But what does it signify, though not one human son should be like his father? Would it prove that the Son of God is not like his Father? By no means. For Christ is "the brightness of God's glory, and the express image of his person." Heb. 1:3. Because Christ is the express image of God's person, he consequently is like his Father. Thus all arguments which can be possibly advanced upon the ground of human generation, can never prove that the Son of God is not like his Father. For since Christ is the express image of God's person, he must necessarily possess all divine perfections; otherwise he could not be the express image of his person: for there would be something in God's person not expressed in the Son, or in this express image. If any man's son were the express image of his person, he certainly would possess all his father's qualities.

Indeed some men, because they have an improper view of the Son's generation, conclude that it is impossible for the Son to be begotten according to his divine personality. They figure to themselves a certain period of time, in which he was begotten like the sons of men. If this supposition were correct, then indeed Christ would have as distinct an existence as any human son had of his father. But it is to be observed that God exists out of time, for he inhabits uncircumscribed eternity; hence if he have an only begotten Son, the express image of his person, his generation has nothing to do with time, but is eternal, immutable, it is the perpetual resplendence of Jehovah's uncreated glory.

Those who deny the eternal generation of the Son upon the supposition of anteriority and posteriority, perhaps do not consider the procession of the Holy Ghost. All Trinitarians as far as I know, acknowledge that the Holy Ghost is a divine person from eternity, without supposing the anteriority of the Father. But does not the Holy Ghost proceed from the Father? This is beyond contradiction, and is I believe admitted by all. Now if the Holy Ghost can proceed from the Father, how is it that the Father is not anterior? Is it not equally rational (if it be rational at all) to believe that a spirit proceeding from God should be posterior to his existence, as to believe a son begotten should be posterior? If there can be an eternal, immutable procession of the Holy Ghost, there also can be an eternal, immutable generation of the Son. If human generation is to be compared to divine generation, and if, because a man's son is posterior to his father, that therefore Christ must be the same in relation to his Father, and if this position be considered conclusive, then may I also with equal force apply the same to the procession of the Holy Ghost. Man was formed out of the dust of the earth before he possessed either breath, or spirit; hence existed prior to his spirit. But will any one assert that the Father existed prior to his Spirit? No. This proves the absurdity of such comparisons. For if the Holy Spirit may proceed eternally from the Father, why may not the Son be eternally begotten?

Although Unitarians deny that the Holy Spirit is a distinct person from the Father; yet their own positions prove that he is from eternity. Some have said that he bears the same relation to God as the spirit of a man to man. Mr. Worcester says, "My ideas of the Spirit may be better understood by a little attention to some Scripture metaphors. ... God is represented by the metaphor of the natural sun. 'The Lord God is a SUN.' Then the *rays* of light and heat, which *emanate* or *proceed* from the sun, are an emblem of the 'Holy Spirit which proceedeth from the Father.' Like the rays of the sun, these Divine emanations of the fullness of God *illuminate, quicken, invigorate,* and *fructify.*" p. 191, 192. Again, "By the Holy Spirit, or the Spirit of God, is not in my view, intended any one attribute merely, but all those attributes which are implied in the FULLNESS OR ALL-SUFFICIENCY OF GOD," p. 192.

Again, "We believe the Holy Ghost, or Holy Spirit was the Spirit of God, and not a person, or being, or substance distinct from God. When communicated to men, it was a supernatural gift, the energy and power of God operating on their minds, giving new light to their understanding, and increasing their natural intelligence and wisdom." *Unitarian Miscellany*, No. 1, vol. 1, p. 17. According to these statements the Holy Ghost is not any one particular divine attribute, but all the attributes implied in the divine fullness, proceeding from the Father. Thus if the Holy Ghost be the fullness of God, must he not be from eternity? Since Unitarians deny that the Holy Ghost is any substance or person distinct from God, they must acknowledge him as well as the Father to be from eternity. Again, if according to Mr. W. the Holy Ghost, like the rays of the sun emanating, proceeds from the Father, then he proceeds eternally; seeing the rays of the sun have emanated from the same ever since its existence. Now if the Holy Ghost eternally proceeds from the Father, without supposing him anterior, why should the eternal generation of the Son suppose the Father's anteriority? Whether the Holy Ghost be called the divine fullness, or a person, it does not essentially affect this argument. Although, it should be admitted that the Holy Ghost is the divine fullness proceeding from God, without being a distinct person; nevertheless he must be something distinct from the Father: for if this Holy Spirit were personally the Father himself, then indeed the Father would proceed from himself. This would be absurd. It is evident that the Holy Ghost is something distinct from the Father, whether this something be a person, or not. This something proceeds eternally from the Father. Now if something distinct from the Father can eternally proceed from him, how can the belief of Christ's eternal generation be absurd?

Some who pass for Trinitarians suppose that Christ is not the Son of God according to his divine nature, but only according to his humanity. Dr. Adam Clarke in his comment of Luke 1:35, says, "Here I trust I may be permitted to say, with all due respect for those who differ from me, that the doctrine of the *eternal Sonship* of Christ is, in my opinion, antiscriptural, and highly dangerous; this doctrine I reject for the following reasons:

"1st. I have not been able to find any *express* declaration in the Scriptures concerning it.

"2dly. If Christ be the Son of God as to his *divine* nature, then he cannot be *eternal*; for *son* implies a *father*; and father implies in reference to *son*, *precedency* in *time*, if not in *nature* too. *Father* and *son* imply the idea of *generation*; and *generation* implies a time in which it *was* effected, and *time* also *antecedent* to such generation.

"3dly. If Christ be the *Son* of God, as to his *divine* nature, then the Father is of necessity *prior*, consequently *superior* to him.

"4thly. Again, if this *divine nature* were *begotten* of the *Father*, then it must be in *time*, i. e. there was a period in which it *did not* exist, and a period when it *began* to exist. This destroys the *eternity* of our blessed Lord, and robs him at once of his Godhead.

"5thly. To say that he was begotten from all *eternity*, is in my opinion absurd; and the phrase, *eternal son*, is a positive self-contradiction. Eternity is that which has had no beginning, nor stands in any reference to time. Son supposes *time, generation* and *father*; and time also *antecedent* to such generation. Therefore the conjunction of these two terms *son* and *eternity* is absolutely impossible, as they imply essentially different and opposite ideas.

"The enemies of Christ's divinity have in all ages availed themselves of this incautious method of treating this subject, and on this ground, have ever had the advantage of the defenders of the godhead of Christ. This doctrine of the *eternal sonship* destroys the *deity* of Christ; now if his deity be taken away, the whole Gospel scheme of redemption is ruined. On this ground, the atonement of Christ cannot have been of *infinite* merit, and consequently could not purchase pardon for the offences of mankind, nor give any right to, or possession of, an *eternal* glory. The very use of this phrase is both absurd and dangerous; therefore let all those who value *Jesus* and their *salvation* abide by the Scriptures."

According to these positions, Christ is not the Son of God as to his divine nature. Notwithstanding, Mr. Clarke supposes that Christ is true eternal God, a distinct person from the Father. But Christ is called the *only begotten* of the Father. John 1:14, 18; 3:16. Now it may be asked, whether to be *created* and to be *begotten* are synonymous? If they be synonymous, how then is Christ the only begotten son of God? Is he the only created son? By no means. For there are myriads of intelligent beings, who have been created: such as men and angels called the sons of God. No being in the universe, except Christ, can with propriety be called God's only begotten Son. It is evident that there is a considerable difference between being begotten and created. Christ therefore, in so far as he is the only begotten is by no means a created being. But is not his humanity created? It is derived from the virgin Mary, by the energy of the Holy Ghost. If his humanity as such were God's only begotten Son, then the humanity could not be created. But since his humanity is a created intelligence, how can it as such be the only begotten Son of God? Again, if Christ be the Son of God according to his humanity only, the question may be put: did the Father beget him? Is it not evident that the Holy Ghost came upon the virgin, who conceived by his energy? If only the humanity of Christ were God's only Son, then surely it would have been begotten by the Father: for it would be absurd to suppose a son without also supposing that he was begotten. Since the virgin conceived by the Holy Ghost, the humanity, merely as such, is not the Father's Son; nor do we find that the humanity is ever called the Son of the Holy Ghost. It must be admitted that the humanity in so far as it is personally united to the Word and is one thing with the same, is God's Son. But to suppose that the humanity separately from the divine nature is the Son of God is out of the question, for the reasons already assigned.

The text in Luke 1:35 does not say that Christ is God's Son, only according to his humanity: "The Holy Ghost shall come upon thee, and the power of the Highest shall overshadow thee; therefore also that holy thing, which shall be born of thee, shall be called the Son of God." That the holy thing born of the virgin should be called the Son of God, does not prove that that holy thing should be a mere man. Unless it can be proven that that holy thing was a mere man, it is in vain to urge this text as a proof that the humanity alone is God's Son.

That if Christ be the Son of God as to his divine nature, that the Father must be prior, that generation implies a time in which it was effected, and time also antecedent to such generation, are assertions which prove nothing against Christ's eternal generation. With respect to men there is a time in which a son is begotten. But how does this apply to God and his Son? How does Mr. Clarke know that if Christ be God's Son, that he must be posterior to his Father? Or that there was a time in which he was begotten? By what has he proven it? Is his mere assertion sufficient evidence? Human generation ought not to be compared to divine generation.

That the supposition of Christ's son-ship as to his divine nature is repugnant to his deity is an unfounded conclusion. For the very position that Christ is God's only begotten Son is a conclusive evidence of his Deity. It would be absurd to suppose that God's only Son should be destitute of his nature and perfections.

There are two texts from which if only superficially viewed, it might be concluded that Christ was begotten in time. The one is, "*Thou art* my Son; this day have I begotten thee." Ps. 2:7. The other is, "who is the image of the invisible God, the first-born of every creature." Col. 1:15. Now it is supposed by some that there was a certain day, i. e. period of time, in which Christ was begotten; and that if he be the first-born of every creature, that himself must be a creature. But, it is to be observed that these texts refer to Christ's resurrection. "But God raised him from the dead: and he was seen many days of them which came up with him from Galilee to Jerusalem, who are his witnesses unto the people. And we declare unto you glad tidings, how that the promise which was made unto the fathers, God hath fulfilled the same unto us their children, in that he hath raised up Jesus again; as it is also written in the second psalm, Thou art my Son, this day have I begotten thee." Acts 13:30–33. Since an inspired apostle declares that God fulfilled the words, "Thou art my Son, this day have I begotten thee," in having raised up Jesus from the dead, it is readily understood that his resurrection is also called a begetting, and the day when he arose was the day referred to by the psalm. One thing is, Christ being the only begotten of God from eternity, or in so far as he is God reflected, or the resplendence of his glory; but another is when, after his incarnation, he is begotten from the dead, when raised up into an endless life. With respect to the text in Col. 1:15, it must be observed that its context shews that Christ is the first-born of every creature in regard to his resurrection. See v. 17, 18: "And he is before all things, and by him all things consist. And he is the head of the body, the church: who is the beginning, the first-born from the dead; that in all things he might have the pre-eminence." Thus it is plain that his resurrection is called a birth. Christ is truly also a creature as well as the creator; so that it may be said that he is the first-born of every creature; seeing that he is the first fruits of those that slept. I Cor. 15:20.

SECTION IV

Some of the principal objections of the Unitarians examined.

One of the principal objections alleged by the Unitarians against the Deity of Christ they endeavor to found on the following text: "And he said unto him, why callest thou me good, there is none good but one, that is God." Matth. 19:19. On this Mr. J. Miller observes, p. 83, "When Christ said why callest thou me good? there is none good but one, that is God; can it reasonably be understood that he meant himself, or that the term included himself as very and eternal God, with two other persons, each of whom was God, independent and supreme?" etc.

Answer. Christ does not say that he is not good, but asked the ruler why he called him good; neither did Christ deny that he was God, but affirmed that God only was good. If the scribe had believed that Christ was God, he might have replied to Christ's question, "Why callest thou me good?" that he called him good, because he believed that he was God. But on supposition that the scribe had denied his Godhead, then his language would have been erroneous; seeing none is good but God. Christ in asking this question, neither denies nor affirms that he is good. Since the answer of the scribe (if he had made any) is not recorded, by what method can it be proven that he disclaimed being good? If a man were to call me a very wise man, and if I would ask him: why he called me so, I would thereby neither deny, nor affirm his assertion. I would only demand his reasons for such an assertion. Had the scribe believed the Godhead of Christ, his address would have been correct according to his belief. Now if on supposition Christ is not God, would he have had asked him: why callest thou me good? For this question would not have robbed him of his opinion, i. e. that Christ is God. Christ in that case with a view to correct such an error, would in all probability have made a different reply. But if, on the contrary, the scribe had denied the Godhead of Christ, then his address would have been ironical. Now in that case, Christ's question, "why callest thou me good?," would have been pertinent to the point.

By such texts as speak of limited and created qualities in the person of Christ, of his humiliation and his exaltation, Unitarians endeavor to prove that Christ is not God. When they have proven that Christ has limited properties—such as ignorance with respect to the time of the judgment day, dependence on his father—and because he suffered and died, they presume that they have sufficiently proven that Christ is not God, seeing it is repugnant to God's nature to be limited, and to suffer and to die. They manifestly, principally build their superstructure upon this datum: *Christ possessed limited* and created qualities; but God is unlimited and uncreated; therefore Christ is not God. If such a position be correct, I might in a similar manner prove that all men are void of sense, memory and judgment. I would arrange the argument thus: All men are formed out of the earth, but earth possesses neither sense, nor memory nor judgment; therefore all men are without sense, memory, and judgment. But would not all Unitarians, as well as all other rational men explode this as a barefaced sophism? For it might properly be replied: that all men being formed out of the earth does not prove that they are without reason; unless it be shewn that men possess nothing else but an earthly body. The position of Unitarians is similar, and stands thus: Christ possessed the infirmities of human nature, sin excepted; he suffered and died; God is omnipotent and immutable; therefore Christ is not God. But this is a sophism. Forasmuch as Christ having possessed the infirmities of humanity, does by no means prove that he has no other nature, nor qualities; and until it be shewn positively that he possesses no other qualities except those which are peculiar to human nature, it is in vain to urge the human qualities possessed by him as an objection against his Deity.

I shall investigate some of those objections severally. The Unitarians say: 1. That the doctrine of two natures is a main prop in the edifice of the trinity. "It represents him (Christ) as speaking in two characters, sometimes as God, sometimes as man, without intimating in which character. Pursue this notion to its consequences; as man he might be mistaken like other men; he has in no single instance given a hint by which we can be certain in which character he spoke, but he uniformly acted and conversed as one being, possessed of one nature, and sustaining one character. By what rule shall we judge? One reads his words, and says it is God that speaks; another says it is man. Who shall decide? Or how shall it be proved that he did not utter the language, and speak with the wisdom of man only, when he published the doctrine of a future state, or any other of the doctrines of revelation. Do you say, that the divine nature always controlled the human in these cases? How do you know? You can only decide by your arbitrary opinion, and every man may do the same, etc." *Unitarian Miscel.* No. 17. p. 33. Again p. 34: "Trinitarians are apt to dwell much on the humility of Christ in descending from the glory of the heavens, taking up his abode with men, submitting to the pains and hardships, etc." Then conclude, "But how can they talk of the humility of the unchangeable God? Can the Being, who is the same from everlasting to everlasting, and whose perfections are as immutable as his nature, can such a being humble himself, lay aside his attributes, and take upon him the nature of a frail, sinful man? etc."

Unitarians readily perceive that if it be shewn that Christ possesses two natures in one person, their principal objections will vanish; consequently, in order to maintain their ground, they deny that he possesses two natures. But upon this principle, how can they answer the question which our Saviour had put to the Pharisees? I presume the Unitarians can as little answer it as the Pharisees. "While the Pharisees were gathered together, Jesus asked them, saying, what think ye of Christ? Whose son is he? They say unto him, The *son* of David. He saith unto them, How then doth David in spirit call him Lord, saying, the Lord said unto my Lord, sit thou on my right hand, till I make thine enemies thy footstool? If David then call him Lord, how is he his son? And no man was able to answer him a word, etc." Matth. 22:41-46. Whereas Christ is both David's Lord and son, he by all means possesses two natures. As David's Lord he is superior to him, but in so far as he is his son he possesses David's nature. David was a true man, Christ is his son; therefore Christ is also a true man. Christ is not only David's Lord but the Lord from heaven, 1 Cor. 15:47. A mere son of David, i. e. a mere man, cannot be the Lord from heaven. It is abundantly evident from the Scriptures, and also admitted by Unitarians, that God created the worlds by Christ; consequently, he exists before creation; hence prior to David, possessing a sublimer nature than that which he derived from David, since his incarnation. Or, indeed is it possible for any one to imagine, that Christ as a mere man born of the virgin Mary about four thousand years after the creation, could have been with respect to this nature before creation, and have created all things? Such a supposition contradicts itself, and I presume no Unitarian maintains it. It is manifest that Christ existed before he was made the son of David. Now if Christ existed before the foundation of the world, did he, or did he not, possess a nature? If he had no nature, then he was a non-entity. But to suppose this, would be an absurdity; hence, surely he had a nature. But did he then possess David's nature? No. For David was not before the foundation of the world. But what nature did Christ possess after he was made David's son? By all means he had David's nature: for every son possesses the nature of his father. Thus since Christ exists before all creation, he has a sublimer nature than that of a mere man, and yet since he afterwards was made David's son, he also possesses man's nature; consequently he has two natures.

That Christ has two natures I shall illustrate in the following remarks. St. Paul says, "Whose are the fathers, and of whom as concerning the flesh Christ *came*, who is over all, God blesses for ever. Amen." Rom. 9:5. If Christ, as concerning the flesh, came of the fathers, then it is manifest that he in some other respect is not of the fathers. It would be absurd to affirm with respect to any mere man, that he came of human parents according to the flesh, forasmuch as that would be necessarily understood without such addition. Hence, when it is said that Christ as concerning the flesh came of the fathers, it is readily understood that he has another nature which is not derived from the fathers. This text does not only prove that Christ derived a nature from the fathers, but also that he is supreme God: *"who is over all, God blessed forever."* It is in vain to suppose that the phrase "God blessed for ever," has reference to God the Father, implying a form of thanksgiving, and that the substantive verb be ought to be understood, so that the sense would be, "Christ is over all, therefore God the Father be blessed forever. Amen." For the original is θεος ευλογητος. ευλογητος is no participle, but an adjective. Adjectives do not, like participles, imply time; hence it is impossible according to correct criticism, to construe this phrase, "God be blessed for ever." It is said that Christ is over all; if so, then he is supreme God: for no being can be above all things, except God.

"And the Word was made flesh." John 1:14. This Word who was made flesh, was in the beginning, he was with God, and he was God, and all things were made by him. v. 1, 2, 3. The term *Word* is used for Son, for it is said of him, "and we beheld his glory, the glory as of the only begotten of the Father, full of grace and truth." This Word existed before the foundation of the world, consequently prior to his incarnation. Thus this text also shews that Christ possesses two natures: the one he has before creation, and the other he assumed in the fullness of time. What the apostle in this text denominates *flesh*, is in other passages called *man*. "For there is one God and one mediator between God and man, the man Christ Jesus." I Tim. 2:5. "And being found in fashion as a man." Phil. 2:8. If Christ be a man, then he by all means possesses man's nature.

He was made like unto his brethren: "Wherefore it behooved him to be made like unto his brethren," etc. Heb. 2:17. He that was made in all things like unto his brethren, must possess our nature. Christ not only possesses human flesh and blood, but also all whatsoever pertains to man's nature: such as a human soul and intelligence. Notwithstanding, he having our nature, yet he is without sin, seeing sin is no constituent part of man's nature. It [that is, sin] is a wrong disposition of the heart, or a volition which is contrary to God's law.

It is said by St. Luke that the child Jesus "increased in wisdom and stature, and in favor with God and man." ch. 2:52. The divine fullness in Christ was not susceptive of increasing in wisdom, stature and favor with God and man; because that is eternally and immutably perfect. If Christ had only a human body, he might have increased in stature, but not in wisdom: for wisdom cannot exist without an intelligent faculty. Hence to increase in wisdom, presupposes a created intelligent faculty. Christ has a soul; for he says, "my soul is exceeding sorrowful, even unto death." Matth. 25:38.

Christ does not only possess our nature, but it is also of the same origin: "for both he that sanctifieth and they who are sanctified *are* all of one: for which cause he is not ashamed to call them brethren." Heb. 2:11. Although the manner of Christ's birth was different from that of other men, nevertheless the genealogies as recorded by the Evangelists sufficiently evince that he is of Adam's race. If Christ, according to the flesh, did not as well as his brethren descend from Adam (Luke 3:23, 38), then God's design under the Old Testament dispensation would have been nullified. In vain he would have preserved the Hebrews a distinct people from all others, and their correct genealogy, so that the Messiah might be recognized as an offspring of Abraham, of Judah, of David agreeably to the divine promise and prediction. Neither could any valid reason be assigned why the Hebrews received more particular favors than all other nations, provided the Messiah had not descended from them: for had they been cut off like other nations, or intermixed with their conquerors, his line of descent would have been destroyed, and God's promises and predictions nullified. Had it been God's design that the Messiah should be a man only, without any regard to his origin, he might, like Adam, have been made out of a lump of clay, and had the breath of life breathed into his nostrils; but since this has not been the case, it is manifest that he is not only a man, but a man of Adam's race.

From the preceeding observations it is evident that Christ possesses two natures. Unitarians can by no means deny that Christ possesses flesh and blood, even if they do not admit that he possesses a human intelligence, or a perfect human nature consisting of a soul and body distinct from his pre-existent nature. Neither have I discovered in any of their writings that they deny that Christ possesses flesh and blood. Since the Scriptures ascribe to Christ divine titles, omnipotent power and infinite dominion, Unitarians suppose that he (notwithstanding they deny that he is God) possesses such by the divine fullness dwelling in his person. In short, they admit that Christ has the Father's fullness. Mr. Worcester (in his *Bible News*, p. 75, 76) admits that Christ is almighty by the indwelling of the Father, or the fullness of the Godhead. Mr. J. Miller also admits that all the fullness of the Godhead dwells in Christ bodily, and that God was manifested in the flesh. (See his letters to Isaac Lewis, p. 45.) The word *fullness* implies that which does not lack any thing, or is a repletion: for if the least should be wanting there can be no fullness. St. Paul says, "when the fullness of the time was come, God sent forth his Son, etc." Gal. 4:4. Like as the fullness did not exclude any part of the time prior to the birth of Christ, even so the fullness of the Godhead cannot exclude any thing pertaining to God: whether it be of substance or attributes. If any thing whatever pertaining to the eternal Godhead should be wanting, then surely there could not be a fullness of the Godhead. The divine essence, the attributes of eternity, infinity, omnipotence, etc. are necessarily included in the divine fullness: for otherwise the Godhead would not be replete. It is not only said that the divine fullness dwells in Christ, but that the Father himself is in him. "The Father, that dwelleth in me, he doeth the works." John 14:10. Since the Father himself dwells in Christ, it is evident that the divine fullness implies every thing pertaining to the Godhead: otherwise the Father himself would not be the eternal Godhead.

The Father's fullness did not dwell in Christ only occasionally, so that it sometimes was separated from his person. Christ is the brightness of the Father's glory: consequently he is God, the eternal, uncreated light reflected. Now if the Father ever had ceased to reflect himself, Christ would also have ceased to exist, because he is this divine luminous reflection. If the Father's fullness had ever left Christ, then he would also have ceased to reflect himself in Christ's person: for the divine fullness is all that whatsoever pertains to the eternal Godhead. Therefore, the divine fullness is essential to Christ's own existence; so that without this fullness it could not properly be said that Christ was Christ. He says, "All things that the Father hath are mine: therefore said I that he shall take of mine and shall shew unto you." John 16:15. If all things that the Father hath are Christ's, then surely the Father's fullness must also be Christ's fullness. If not, then Christ's assertion "that all things that the Father hath are his," could not be justified: for the Father has a divine fullness; Christ has the very, the same, fullness. Therefore Christ, even in his sufferings, was not without the Father. When he was about to enter into his sufferings he said, "Behold the hour cometh, yea is now come, that ye shall be scattered, every man to his own, and shall leave me alone: and yet I am not alone, because the Father is with me." John 16:32. Again, "God was in Christ reconciling the world unto himself." 2 Cor. 5:17. Thus it is evident that the Father never was separated from Christ, even not in his sufferings.

Since it has been proven that Christ possesses two natures, it is hence evident that he also possesses two different kinds of properties. The divine nature is not without divine properties, such as omnipotence, omniscience, etc. Neither is the human nature without human properties; such as being limited in knowledge and power, subject to mortality, etc. Since Christ possesses both divine and human properties in one person, the Scriptures properly ascribe to him not only divine works and prerogatives: but also human weakness; such as limited knowledge, sorrows, pains and even death; and also an inferiority to, and a dependence upon, his Father.

The objection that it cannot be known when Christ speaks

as God, and when he speaks as man, can only properly be urged against those Trinitarians who deny that the natures in Christ are so deeply and inseparably united, that the properties of each (yet without mixture or confusion) flow together in the same person. As if when Christ speaks as being almighty, this only should belong to the divine nature, or when he speaks of sufferings and death, it should simply mean that a mere man suffered and died, then he would speak in a twofold character, or as two persons; consequently, it could not always be known when he speaks as God, and when as man. But the two natures are one person; consequently, whatsoever Christ speaks and does, he speaks and does as a person. Thus when he says, that he does not know all things—i. e. the hour and day of the last judgment in his state of humiliation—it is not merely human nature that speaks, but Christ the God-man. But it can be plainly shewn that some of Christ's properties and actions originate, or flow, from one nature only; notwithstanding, the other nature partakes of the same properties and actions because of the inseparable personal union. St. Paul says, that "Christ was made of the seed of David according to the flesh, and declared *to be* the Son of God with power, according to the spirit of holiness by the resurrection from the dead." Rom. 1:3, 4. This shews how one thing ascribed to the person, is the property of one nature only. The text does not say that the flesh only was made of the seed of David, but Christ. The word *Christ* does not denote one or the other nature only. For if either nature could be called Christ, then there would be two Christs, which is contrary to the Scriptures. *Christ* is a personal appellation including the two natures. But how was he of the seed of David, when he had an eternal pre-existence? The apostle says that he was of the seed of David according to the flesh. It is the property of the flesh to be derived from David; yet it is properly said that Christ is of the seed of David, because his flesh is one thing with himself, for the Word was made flesh; hence whatsoever may be the properties and actions of the flesh, the divine nature is a partaker of the same.

Again, St. Peter says, "For Christ also hath once suffered for sins, the just for the unjust, that he might bring us to God, being put to death in the flesh, but quickened by the Spirit." 1 Epist. 3:18. The flesh only is subject to mortality; whereas the divine nature in itself is immortal. The human nature of itself possesses no quickening power; hence to quicken is a work peculiar to divine nature. Nevertheless, the flesh and the divine nature are one person; consequently, if the flesh died, the Godhead was a partaker of this death because this flesh and blood of Christ is God's own flesh and blood. It is not only said that he took part of flesh and blood, Heb. 2:14, but also that "God purchased his church with his own blood." Acts 20:28.

St. Peter does not say that the flesh only was put to death, but that Christ was put to death in the flesh: for the flesh of itself is not Christ. If the flesh only had been put to death, then the reading of the text would have to be "the flesh was put to death in the flesh," which would be absurd. But since it reads, Christ was put to death in the flesh, the indication is that Christ as a person suffered and died according to his flesh, since the flesh was subject to mortality, and yet a constituent part of this divine person. If I were to say that a certain man had been wounded in his arm, I undoubtedly would be understood that the wound was not immediately received by any other member of the body; but yet, that the man himself had been wounded, because his arm is a part of himself. If the flesh be a part of Christ, and that died, then surely Christ personally died, since that which is a part of himself died.

Unitarians ask, "Can the Being who is the same from everlasting to everlasting, and whose perfections are as immutable as his nature, can such a being humble himself, lay aside his attributes, and take upon him the nature of a frail, sinful man?"

Answer. No well informed Trinitarian supposes that the Son of God as God, or according to his divine nature, had ever humbled himself. When in the fullness of time he assumed human nature, he could then in this, or according to this nature, humble himself without a change in his divine essence. For it must be admitted that the human nature was most superlatively exalted by the eternal filial Godhead being assimilated to the same. The Godhead is immutable; hence the humanity did not render it higher nor lower. But the humanity is a changeable nature, it was therefore susceptible of being exalted and glorified with an uncreated divine glory by reason of the eternal Word having become one person with the same. Consequently, God's Son could humble himself according to the humanity.

It is in vain to ask, how God (i. e. the Son) could lay aside his attributes? as I do not believe that he had ever laid them aside. To have laid his attributes aside would suppose that he had changed and become destitute of such attributes. That he took upon himself human nature, and its infirmities—sin excepted—does not prove that he must also have laid aside his attributes. The human nature having been received into his person neither changes nor annihilates his divine nature. Is it impossible for God to take a human nature upon himself? Can such an impossibility be proven? Those who deny that God could take upon himself human nature ought by all means to prove it. Merely to ask how the immutable God could take upon him the nature of a frail, sinful man is no proof that he could not, nor that he did not take upon him human nature. I have not discovered in any of the writings of Unitarians that they offer any proof either from the works of nature or from the Scriptures that it is impossible for God to take upon him human nature. Let them do it if they be able; and if they succeed in it, they will utterly overthrow the doctrine of Christ's eternal Godhead. But until they do this, it is in vain to say that it is absurd to believe that God could take upon him the nature of man.

2. Mr. Worcester observes, "But there is another argument which, if possible, is still more weighty, to which we may now attend. You cannot be insensible that it is plainly and abundantly represented in the Scriptures, the SON of God did *really* and *personally suffer* and *die* for us. And that on this ground both the love of God and the love of his SON are represented as having been manifested in a very extraordinary manner. And if the SON of God be *truly* the SON of God, a derived intelligence, these representations may be strictly and affectingly true. For on this hypothesis the SON of God may be the same intelligent Being as the soul of the Man Christ Jesus who suffered on the cross.

"But your theory will not, I suspect, be found to admit, or support, any thing more than the *shadow* of the *suffering* and *death* of the SON OF GOD.

"Writers and preachers on your side of the question, do, indeed, often speak of the *abasement*, the *sufferings*, and *death*, of the Son of God, as though they believed these things to be affecting realities.

But, after all, what is the amount of these representations, upon your hypothesis? You do not conceive that the Son of God became united to flesh and blood as the soul of Jesus Christ. So far from this, you suppose that the Son of God was personally the self-existent God; and instead of becoming the soul of a human body, you suppose he became mysteriously united to a proper man, who, as distinct from the Son of God, had a true body and reasonable soul. And I think, Sir, it will be found that on this *Man* your theory lays the iniquities of us all; that this *Man*, and not the Son of God, endured the stripes by which we have healing. For while you maintain that the Son was personally the only living and true God, you very consistently affirm 'he did not suffer in the least in his Divine nature, but altogether in his human nature.' And what is this but affirming that he did not suffer at all as the *Son of God*, but only the *Man Jesus* suffered, to whom the Son was united? As, on the Athanasian hypothesis, the *Man* Christ Jesus and the *human nature* are the same. You suppose the SON as incapable of suffering as the Father, and that he did not in *reality* suffer on the cross any more than the Father did; nor any more than either of them suffered while Cranmer was burning at the stake. How, then, does it appear that 'God spared not his own Son.'

"You will probably plead that the *Man* Jesus was united to the *Person* of the Son of God and that *Person suffered* in his *human nature*. But, Sir, as you predicate personality on the *Son* or *Divine nature*, and do not allow personality to the *human nature*, it will, I suspect, be difficult for you to prove that *any Person* suffered on the *cross*: for the sufferings fell simply on a *nature* to which you do not allow personality. As in your view the Son was the self-existent God, and could not suffer in his *Divine* nature, HE could not *suffer* in *any* nature. The man was only an appendage to his Person, mysteriously connected; and yet so far was the union from being very intimate or essential, that the *appendage* or the *Man* might suffer the severest agonies, and the *Son* or *real Person* be at the same time in a state of infinite felicity." Bible News, p. 67–69.

Again he says, "It has been, and I think justly, supposed that the dignity of the Son of God gave value to the sufferings of the cross. And if we consider the Son of God to be what his title imports, a derived Intelligence of Divine origin and dignity, the one by whom

God created the world; if we consider this self-same Intelligence as *personally* and *really suffering the death of the cross*, we may perceive something, in view of which we may well exclaim, 'Behold what manner of love!'

"But if the sufferings of the cross did not *really* fall on that very Son who had sustained pre-existent glory in the 'form of God,' but on a man who had existed less than forty years, who had acted in public character not more than four or five, how small the degree of *condescension* on the part of the *sufferer*, how small the display of the *love* of God, and of what diminished value are the sufferings of the cross! In the Assembly's Catechism we are taught, that 'Christ's humiliation consisted in his being born, and that in a low condition, being made under the law; undergoing the miseries of this life, the wrath of God, and the cursed death of the cross; in being buried, and continuing under the power of death for a time.'

Yet this same catechism teaches us to believe that Jesus Christ was personally the self-existent God. I will then ask, whether there be one particular of what is said respecting the humiliation of Christ, which can *possibly be true*? Was the self-existent God ever born? Was he ever in a low condition? Was he ever made under the law? Did he ever suffer the wrath of God, or the cursed death of the cross? Was God ever buried? —If the self-existent God has not passed through such scenes, then the SON of God has not, according to your doctrine respecting the Son. Therefore, according to your theory, all the *abasement*, which can be supported, falls on the *Man* to which the Son was united: And this *Man* you suppose had no existence until he was conceived in the womb of the virgin Mary; of course, he had no glory to leave, or lay aside when he came into the world. As he never had been *rich*, it was impossible for him to become *poor* for our sake. He had no opportunity to say, 'Lo I come to do thy will, O God.' And so far as his humiliation consisted in 'being born, and that in a low condition,' there was nothing voluntary in it; and it could be no evidence of any love or condescension in him.

"To make out your theory of the humiliation and abasement of the Son of God, you have to take into view two distinct intelligent Beings; one of which you affirm to be the self-existent God, and the other a proper Man. This God, or Son of God, you find had been in a state of pre-existent dignity and glory; and he, as you suppose, was united mysteriously to a Man; this Man was born in low circumstances, endured the miseries of this life, and suffered death on the cross; and by virtue of his union to the Son of God, he was enabled to bear a vastly greater weight of suffering than he could otherwise have endured.

"But, Sir, is this all that is intended by God's SPARING NOT HIS OWN SON? Is this the way in which the SON of God BARE our sins in his OWN BODY on the tree? What, sir, was the *real condition* of the SON of God, the self-existent God, from the birth of the Man Jesus till this Man rose again from the dead? According to your theory, the SON of God, during the whole of that period, was in a state of infinite glory and felicity, and as incapable of suffering the agonies of death as the Father. How then can it be true, that 'Though a SON, yet learned he obedience by the things which HE SUFFERED?' As it respects the *real character* of the SUFFERING SAVIOUR, what is your theory better than Socinianism enveloped in mystery?" *Bible News*, p. 70–72.

Answer. Does Mr. Worcester suppose, when he asserts that Trinitarians maintain that Christ is personally the self-existent God, that they believe that Christ is God without the Father? If there should be any Trinitarian that has ever expressed such an idea, I hereby contradict and disavow such an opinion. I believe that Christ is truly God, but neither of, nor by, himself. He is God by the Father. If he were God without the Father, he would also be a distinct being from him. But as Christ neither exists, nor is, God without the Father, all such objections, which are calculated to confound the distinctive relations between the Father and Son, are urged in vain. As, for instance, Mr. J. Miller says, "If there be no God besides Jesus Christ, what Father is he equal with? Has the one eternal God an equal Father? Should it be answered that the one eternal God has no Father, with whom he is equal, and yet that the one eternal God is equal with the Father, I must answer that such language to me is unintelligible.

"Does not equality imply distinction and plurality, and is it not contrary to all analogy and language, to declare a being equal with himself? Were there but one man in existence, could he have an equal? And if there be but one supreme God who is an infinite Spirit, can there be another equal to him?" p. 128.

Answer. I do not say that there is another God distinct from Christ, nor that he is a distinct God from the Father. I have already shewn that the Father is an eternal uncreated light, and that Christ is the brightness thereof. Now it is self-evident that a light and its brightness are not two lights; therefore the Father and Christ are not two supreme Beings. But a light and its brightness, though substantially the same, have different modes of existence: for the brightness being the light reflected, exists in the mode of reflection, and is thus distinguished from the light. Christ, though possessing the Father's substance, yet he has a different mode* of existence: for he exists in the mode of reflection; so that the distinction between the Father and Christ may easily be discerned. Christ is not only distinguished from the Father in this respect, but also with respect to his incarnation: for in the fullness of time he assumed a human nature. The Father was not made flesh. Neither can it be said that the eternal Godhead was made flesh in the Father's mode of existence; but it was truly made flesh in the Son's mode of existence, that is, God in so far as he is reflected, or properly the divine resplendence, i.e. the Son was made flesh. Thus it may be said that the Father is an invisible light, independent and self-existent, not only with respect to his substance, but also with respect to the mode of his existence; <u>hence his nature</u> is nothing but God; whereas Christ truly possesses

---

* When I say that Christ exists in a different mode from the Father, I do not wish to be understood as if the three persons merely existed in a three-fold mode, without also being truly distinct. For thus there might be only one person in God, who at different times might manifest himself in different modes. This would be *Sabellianism*. Noctus in the third century taught that there is one independent divine being having three distinct names, viz: that of Father, Son and Holy Ghost, who as the Father gave the law under the Old Testament dispensation, and as the Son under the New became incarnate, and afterwards as the Holy Ghost came upon the apostles. Hence according to this the Father would have suffered. Consequently his followers were called *Patripassiani* and *Theopaschitae*. This same doctrine a few years afterwards was renewed by *Sabellius*. Thus the *Theopaschitae* or *Sabellians* only taught a Trinity in name, but not of persons.

I believe three distinct persons in God. But it must be observed that there is a difference between affirming that God merely exists in a three-fold mode, without distinct persons, and that these three distinct persons, each of whom having a peculiar mode of existence.

the Father's substance, yet his mode of existence is eternally and perpetually caused by the Father, i. e., he is reflected by the Father; or he is the resplendence of the invisible God, and the express image of his person, and has assumed a human nature, which the Father does not personally possess. Now Christ, because he is distinct in personality, may be equal with the Father without supposing a plurality of Gods, nor that the self-same person should be equal with himself. Objections of this kind are founded upon the supposition that there is no distinction between the supreme Being and divine persons. But when the distinction between the Father's and Christ's persons is shewn, then it may easily be understood how Christ may have a father, be begotten, and sent and anointed by him, without supposing that the same person should be his own father, be begotten, sent and anointed by himself.

Mr. Worcester, in the above quotation, argues against those Trinitarians who suppose that nothing more than the human nature of Christ suffered and died. Although he does not believe that Christ is God, yet he supposes that he has a sublimer nature than that of a mere man, which existed before his incarnation. He maintains that not only an appendage of Christ, but that he personally suffered and died. His arguments against those who suppose that a mere man died, in so far as they respect Christ's personal sufferings and death, it must be confessed are cogent and conclusive. But it must be observed that not all Trinitarians maintain that a mere man suffered and died. Lutherans in particular utterly disavow such an opinion. They believe that Christ, hence not a mere man, suffered and died.

Those who assert that Christ is God, and yet declare that nothing more than a human nature suffered and died, contradict themselves in a most glaring manner. For if they be asked whether Christ suffered and died, they will answer in the affirmative. If they be asked: "Who is Christ?," their answer will be, "He is the Son of God, true God and man in one person." Now if they be asked whether his divine nature, or Godhead, also was a partaker of sufferings and death, they will answer, "By no means: for that would be impossible." Thus the contradiction is manifest. For if Christ suffered and died, and if he be God and man in one person, how could Christ ever have suffered and died, unless a God-man had suffered and died? To affirm that Christ died, and yet to assert that nothing but a human nature died, is virtually saying that Christ is nothing more than a human nature. This is truly denying Christ's Godhead, even by those who otherwise seem to contend for it. Why do such not speak consistently? If they cannot believe that the Godhead of Christ could be a partaker of sufferings and death, why do they not at once deny that he is God, when they must acknowledge that Christ suffered and died. Whatever Christ may be, the same must have been a partaker of sufferings and death. Was he a mere man? Then a man only suffered and died. Was he a sublime spirit, superior to any of the angels joined to a human body? Then such a spirit was a partaker of sufferings and death. Was he God reflected, or the brightness of the Father's glory made flesh? Then this filial Godhead suffered and died in flesh.

The Scriptures declare that when Christ was crucified, a greater one than man was crucified. St. Paul declares, "But we speak the wisdom of God in a mystery, *even* the hidden *wisdom*, which God ordained before the world unto our glory: which none of the princes of this world knew: for had they known it, they would not have crucified the Lord of glory." 1 Cor. 2:7, 8. Again, St. Peter says, "But ye denied the Holy One and the Just, and desired a murderer to be granted unto you; and killed the Prince of life, whom God hath raised from the dead, etc." Acts 3:14, 15. Can a mere man be the Lord of glory, and the Prince of life? *The Lord of glory* and *Prince of life*, are divine titles and cannot be attributed to a mere creature. The apostles expressly declare that the Lord of glory and Prince of life had been crucified and killed; hence not a mere man joined to God's Son. Or indeed, will any Trinitarian who denies that Christ died in the full sense of the word attempt to prove that the mere humanity of Christ was the Lord of glory and the Prince of life? If this can be done, I wish to see it attempted. But I presume no Trinitarian of the aforesaid opinion would assay to prove that the titles *Lord of glory* and *Prince of life* belong to a mere creature: for thereby he would surrender one of his arguments in behalf of the Godhead of Christ, as it is argued that the title *Lord* answers to the Hebrew Jehovah, which title is not attributed to a mere creature, but properly belongs to the supreme God.

I would ask those Trinitarians whether Christ was God or a mere man whilst he was dead? If they acknowledge that he was God whilst dead, then they must also acknowledge that the Godhead was a partaker of death. But if they deny that he was God whilst he was dead, then they must also deny that he had the power to raise himself up from the dead, and thus contradict the Scriptures. For how could a mere man raise himself from the dead? It requires the same power to raise a dead person as to create a world. Although it be said that the Father raised Christ from the dead, yet did he also raise himself: for he laid down his life, that he might take it again; he had power to lay it down, and he had power to take it again. John 10:17, 18. Again Christ said, "The Son can do nothing of himself, but what he seeth the Father do: for what things soever he doeth, these also doeth the Son likewise." John 5:19. Now if Christ laid down his life that he might take it again, it is plain that he raised himself up from the dead. Moreover, since the Father raised up Christ; consequently he, because what things soever the Father doeth these he also doeth likewise, must have raised himself. Had the Godhead of Christ been separated from the humanity in death, then the Godhead would have been a distinct person from the humanity; hence had the Godhead thus separated, even raised the humanity, it could by no means be said that he raised himself, but the Son of God would only have raised up a mere man, with whom he at that time had no personal connection. But as the Scriptures plainly shew that Christ raised himself, he must have been God-man even in death. Can one be raised from the dead, provided he be not dead? By no means. Could a God-man have raised himself, provided a mere man, but not a God-man, had been dead? By no means. Since Christ raised himself from the dead, it is evident that his Godhead, even in death, was not separated from his humanity. But if it be asked how he could have been dead, provided his divine nature had not been separated, it may be answered: in the same as the souls of men animate their bodies, even so the human soul of Jesus animated his body; consequently, in death his soul and body were separated, whereas his Godhead in the meanwhile was inseparably united with his dead body and disembodied soul. Now since the separation of the soul from the body is death, and as Christ's Godhead was one thing with his body and soul, it must follow that the same was a partaker of death. Christ at the same time was both immortal and mortal. He is immortal in so far as he is God and mortal in so far as he assumed human nature. The humanity, because the Word was made flesh, is the filial Godhead's own humanity; consequently its weakness and mortality had become the weakness and mortality of this Godhead. Although the humanity being inseparably one thing with the Godhead could not change the same, yet the humanity in this oneness yielded to the Godhead its weakness and mortality, of which the Godhead otherwise would have been destitute. I do not say that the Godhead of Christ died according to the Godhead, but that the humanity having yielded its weakness and mortality to the Godhead, the same was a partaker of death. Thus indeed did Christ in the midst of death possess immortality; and yet, because, he assumed a weak and mortal nature which suffered and died, it is evident that this divine person was truly a partaker of death, or as St. Peter expresses it, "he was put to death in the flesh."

Because Christ humbled himself, was crucified, dead and buried, Unitarians suppose that he is not God; seeing that God is unchangeable, and can therefore not be subject to any abasement, nor death. But it seems to me—provided, I understand them properly—that this same objection may be urged against their own hypothesis with equal force. I have already shewn that Unitarians acknowledge that all the fullness of the Godhead dwells bodily in Christ, that he is almighty by the indwelling of the Father, etc. Again, from the tenor of the writings of the Unitarians, I understand that they maintain that although he is not God, yet that he performed his miracles by the power of God in him; in short when he acted in a supreme, divine manner, or had all power in heaven and in earth, it was by the indwelling of the Father or his fullness. Now if upon the hypothesis of the Unitarians, the fullness of the Father dwell in him—if he be almighty by the indwelling of the Father—then it must follow that this divine fullness, or the Father himself must be closely united with Christ's person. If not, how could all God's fullness dwell bodily in him? How could he have all power in heaven and in earth, and have performed so many divine works? Neither could this divine fullness have left him even in death. If it had, he could not have raised himself from the dead, which was a miracle, which could not have been effected without omnipotent power. Now if the fullness of God dwelt bodily in Christ, I would ask Unitarians, when Christ abased himself, when he suffered and died, was not also this fullness abased, did it not suffer and die? It has already been shewn that the divine fullness includes all God's essence, and perfections; hence the Godhead itself. This God as Unitarians (*correctly*) admit was in Christ; (or all his fullness bodily) and by whose indwelling he performed his miracles; how then shall it otherwise be concluded, than that this Godhead must also have been abased, have suffered and died when Christ was abased, when he suffered and died? could the divine fullness undergo such changes. Thus the same objections Unitarians urge against Trinitarians (in this point) are equally against themselves. If they answer these objections, they have also answered for Trinitarians.

If Unitarians answer that Christ in his state of humiliation did not at all times use his indwelling power, and majesty; or that he was not always assisted by his divine fullness, that therefore he could suffer and die, although he possessed such a fullness, Trinitarians may answer in a similar manner. They may answer since the filial Godhead was made flesh, the humanity is a partaker of divine perfections; hence Christ, in so far as it answered his mediatorial office in his state of humiliation, did not use his Godhead, or he kept back his power and glory. It is readily admitted that if at all times his Godhead had exerted its omnipotence and glory upon him, that he could never have suffered, nor died. That the Godhead of Christ in this state of humiliation did not at all times exert his power in Christ's person does not prove that his Godhead must have been changed. One thing is, that Christ at all times was in possession of his eternal Godhead; but another is, when this Godhead did not at all times exert its omnipotence in his person. Christ according to the flesh was humbled. In order to effect this amazing humiliation, it was not necessary that he should have been divested of his Godhead; it was sufficient if only his Godhead did not at all times exert his power and glory in his person.

If, according to Unitarians, it was possible for all the fullness of the Godhead to dwell bodily in Christ, and yet for him to be humbled, to suffer and to die, without impairing, or changing the divine fullness, then surely there can be nothing absurd in maintaining that since Christ is the filial Godhead made flesh, that he according to the flesh was humbled, and that he suffered and died, without changing his Godhead.

Some suppose that the divine nature of Christ was separated from the humanity when he was suspended on the cross; hence [they] imagine that a mere man died. They presume to prove this from our Saviour's exclamation, "Eloi, Eloi, lama, sabacthani?" Or "My God, My God, why hast thou forsaken me?," Mark 15:34. But it must be observed that the divine personality of Christ is not his own God. The Father is called Christ's God. (See Joh. 20:17.) Christ says, "why hast thou forsaken me?" *Me* is a personal pronoun, and indicates Christ's person. But who can imagine, unless he be blinded, that the mere humanity of Christ was his person, or Christ? It seems thus that not a mere man, but Christ was forsaken of God. It is manifest that these words were spoken in reference to the Father. But the Father, in forsaking Christ, was by no means personally out of Christ: for the contrary position has already been established. To forsake does not always imply a local or a personal separation. God forsakes the wicked and leaves them to the hardness of their hearts; yet who can deny that they as well as others live, move and have their being in him? Acts 17:28. All things are upheld by his power, hence also the wicked; notwithstanding he forsakes them. Now in forsaking the wicked, he is not locally separated from them. I shall by no means decide wherein God forsook Christ; whether he withdrew from him all inward comfort, or whether Christ exclaims, "My God, My God, why hast thou forsaken me?" because he had no help against his enemies. (See Ps. 22.)

Although the Father forsook Christ, yet did Christ also deny himself of happiness and glory for a little season. Christ laid down his own life; he made himself of no reputation and became obedient unto death, even the death of the cross. Phil. 2:8. The Father and Christ having the same omnipotent power, it must follow that when the Father withheld his power in assisting Christ in his suffering, Christ's own power was kept back from succoring himself.

Again, some very confidently assert, that if the divine nature of Christ had been a partaker of sufferings and death, that in the meanwhile universal nature could not have been sustained; that the universe would have been disordered, or annihilated. This objection is urged by some inconsiderate Trinitarians. But are they so blinded that they cannot discriminate the difference between the Father's and the Son's persons? Do they suppose that the Father was also incarnate? Do they not know that the Son only was made flesh, and that the Godhead in this personal distinction suffered according to the flesh?

If the sufferings of the Godhead should cause convulsions in nature, then surely Christ the God-man must have suffered. Were not the most extraordinary convulsions and miracles exhibited at the time of Christ's crucifixion? The earth quaked, the rocks burst, the veil of the temple at Jerusalem was rent, and the sun totally eclipsed. *Dionysius Areopagita* [was] a heathen philosopher; he, when in Egypt, saw an eclipse of the sun, contrary to nature, at the passion of our Saviour Christ and said, "*Aut Deus naturae patitur, aut mundi machina dissolvetur.*" That is, "Either the God of nature suffers, or the frame of the world is about to be dissolved."

Although God did not suffer in his substance, yet was the filial Godhead* so intimately one thing with the flesh, that those extraordinary convulsions and miracles in nature at his death gave the most emphatical signs that more than a mere man was the august sufferer.

The above expression of Dionysius ought to cause many professors of Christianity to blush, who profess Christ as God, and yet maintain that nothing but a mere man suffered and died.

3. Unitarians object [to the teaching] that Christ is God because he said he could do nothing of himself. "If," say they, "he had infinite power, would it be true for him to say, that he *could of himself do nothing?*" John 5:30. (*Unitarian Miscellany*, vol. 1, no. III, page 107.)

Again, they ask, "If the Son possessed in himself all fullness, why should the Father have communicated any assistance to his humanity? Would he not have been personally sufficient of himself?" (See *Bible News*, p. 126-127.)

<u>Answer.</u> Notwithstanding, God upholds all creatures in

---

* By the term filial Godhead, I do not mean a distinct God from the Father, but only the person of the Son, who also has the Father's substance.

their existence; yet they have created faculties. A creature may exert his own abilities, without an immediate exertion of omnipotence. One thing is when God upholds all creatures in their existence; but another is when a creature can act without a supernatural assistance, by reason of his created abilities. For if all a creature would do was also done by the immediate assistance of God, then all the works of the creature would be the works of God, whether they be good or evil. The wicked works a creature does are not done by the assistance of God. If so, God would do the wicked works himself. To assert this would be a blasphemy. Creatures act, not only in some cases with respect to moral, but also with respect to natural actions, in consequence of their created abilities. Now, if Christ could do any thing without the Father, then it would follow that he like the creatures had a separate power and that he would be a distinct being from the Father. But since he can do nothing of himself, but only can act in unity with the Father, it proves that he and the Father have the same uncreated power. The identity of power proves the identity of being. Jesus said, "The Son can do nothing of himself, but what he seeth the Father do: for what things soever he doeth, these also doeth the Son likewise." John 5:19. The Father performed works of omnipotence, Christ performs the same works; hence must possess the same omnipotence. When two persons possess the self-same power, it is manifest that one cannot act with this power, but only in conjunction with the other.

Christ ranks himself with his Father in the performance of divine works. When Jesus performed a miracle on the sabbath, the Jews accused him with having committed a breach of the sabbath-day. He does not deny this charge. But he justifies his conduct in asserting that he done nothing more than his Father also done. "My Father worketh hitherto, and I work." John 5:17. God rested on the seventh day, (i.e. the first sabbath) from all his works. This rest ascribed unto God by Moses, consists in this, that he did not work miraculously as he did in creating the world, (after the first sabbath) but suffers nature to work. Consequently every miracle is a breach of the sabbath which God had sanctified: for it requires the same omnipotence without natural means to perform a miracle as it did to create the world; or, properly speaking, the creating of the world was a miracle. Thus the import of these words is the following: God himself sometimes breaks the greater sabbath, of which the Jewish sabbath is a figure; he did not, when he had completed the works of creation, vow such a rest that he should never be at liberty to work again, but he sometimes works yet, and Christ in conjunction with him. He that speaks as if he with the Father had broken the great sabbath, which was sanctified after the completion of creation, ranks himself with the Father as the creator of the world.

I do not say that Christ possessed all the divine fullness in himself without the Father. The Father's fullness is Christ's fullness. Because the Father's and Christ's power is the same, Christ could not communicate any assistance to his humanity without the Father.

Mr. J. Miller says, "That the Trinitarian theory divides the supreme and indivisible Godhead; so much so, that one part can beget in the person of the Father, another part can be begotten in the person of the Son, and another part can proceed in the person of the Holy Ghost. The represents the Supreme Godhead as being completely divided among three persons, the first begetting, the second begotten, and the third proceeding. Hence it cannot be said of the whole Supreme Godhead, that it was either begetting, begotten, or proceeding; for were the whole begetting in the person of the Father, no part could be begotten in the person of the Son. Were the whole begotten in the person of the Son, no part could beget in the person of the Father, and were the whole proceeding in the person of the Holy Ghost, he could proceed from neither the Father nor the Son." (Page 113.)

Answer. The first section of this treatise partly answers this objection. I have there shewn that the Father is an uncreated light, and that Christ is the brightness thereof. Is it impossible for a luminary to reflect itself without being divided? Is the reflection derogatory to its unity? When a luminary reflects itself, is a part only or the whole luminary reflected? The fact proves that the whole luminary reflects itself, and it is thereby neither divided nor multiplied.

Mr. Miller does not only admit that all the fullness of God dwells in Christ, but also that God gave him all power in heaven and in earth. p. 102. This he urges as an objection against the doctrine of Christ's Godhead. All power in heaven and in earth is nothing less than omnipotence. The almighty power of God is seen by the visible creation, heaven and earth, and all things therein. "For the invisible things of him from the creation of the world are clearly seen, being understood by the things that are made, even his eternal power and Godhead." Rom 1:20. Since the works of creation manifest God's eternal power, it follows that if Christ has all power in heaven and in earth, that he has almighty power. Again, concerning the Father it is said that he is the God of the spirits of all flesh. Numb. 16:22. To be God of the spirits of all flesh implies omnipotence. Jesus has the same power. He says that power was given him over all flesh, that he should give eternal life to as many as were given him. John 17:2. Thus the power in heaven and in earth given to Christ was nothing less than omnipotence.

Now let me ask Mr. M.: Do you believe that there is more than one omnipotent power? Your answer is beyond all doubt in the negative. Had the Father omnipotent power after he had given omnipotent power to Christ? If you say, the Father had no omnipotence after he gave such to Christ, then you would suppose the Father changed and became destitute of omnipotence. This I know you will by no means affirm. But if you say (which you cannot otherwise) that the Father, although he gave Christ all power, yet retained his omnipotence, I would then ask, "Has Christ a separate omnipotence from that of the Father's?" If the Father be omnipotent, and yet, according to your own concession, has given all power in heaven and in earth to Christ, does it not prove that there must be two omnipotent powers—the one in the Father, and the other which he gave to Christ? This conclusion is inevitable upon your theory. For you say that the Father and Christ are separate and distinct beings. If so, they must possess separate and distinct omnipotent powers: for every distinct being has its distinct abilities. It matters not whether Christ derived this almighty power from God or not; it was his own power after it was given to him. According to your belief, Christ derived his existence from the Father; and yet, you suppose him a separate being from the Father. As your theory supposes Christ a separate being from God, it must also suppose that there are two omnipotent powers. Nor, Mr. M., please not to accuse Trinitarians with the doctrine of a plurality of infinities, and other attributes, and even Gods, when your own theory supposes that the Father is omnipotent, and that he also gave omnipotent power to Christ and yet supposes them to be distinct beings. Almighty power is an attribute and prerogative of God. When he appeared to Abram, he said unto him "I am the almighty God; walk before me, and be thou perfect." Gen. 17:1. Hence, he who is almighty is God, seeing he possesses God's attribute and prerogative. Whereas, you admit that Christ received almighty power, you must also admit that Christ, if not by nature, yet that he was made a God, and that too, a distinct God from the Father; hence that there are two Gods. But if you say, with Mr. Worcester, that Christ is almighty by the indwelling of the Father and by his fulness, then you must acknowledge that the Father's power is Christ's power; in short that he has all glory by God's fulness. But if you acknowledge this, you will overthrow your own theory, which supposes Christ a separate being from the Father. For if the Father's power and glory are Christ's power and glory, then they are one being. It is out of the question to suppose that the Almighty power of God could be abstracted from his being, and thus abstracted be given to another. Almighty power cannot exist unless it be in God. If Christ be almighty, the Father must be identified with his person, and consequently they must be one being. *Compare these remarks with what Mr. M. says, page 71.*

    5. Mr. Miller says, "That the Father of Christ is alone the Supreme God, is necessarily inferred from the consideration that Christ offered up prayers and supplications to him."

    Heb. 5:7. "Who in the days of his flesh, when he had offered up prayers and supplications."

    He also quoted John 17:5. Mark 14:36. Luke 23:34. ch. 23:46. He then observes:

    "It was indeed the practice of Christ frequently to address himself in language of supplication to the Father; but in doing this did he not address himself to the Supreme God? Had he made supplication to a God consisting of three co-equal persons, and if he himself was one of the supposed persons, he must as well have supplicated himself as the other persons. But is this an admissible supposition? Does it not involve the most palpable incongruity? If, then, our blessed Saviour addressed himself in his prayers and supplications to but one person, even God his *Father*, does it not necessarily follow that the Father is the Supreme God?

"Christ not only addressed his Father as the one Supreme God, but he also directed his disciples to follow his steps. Matth. 6:9. After this manner, therefore pray ye; Our Father which art in heaven, hallowed be thy name.

"May we not regard this as a safe, an excellent, and perfect model? But to whom is this prayer to be addressed but to the Supreme God? Is it not evident, then, that the Father of Christ is alone the Supreme God? As there is not the least intimation that the disciples were to address three distinct and infinite persons in order to address the Supreme God, but the Father only, is not the idea that the Father alone is the Supreme God as necessary as it is rational? But is not prayer which is addressed to two other persons, each of whom is considered self-existent and Supreme God, an essential departure from this perfect model? Does it not imply an egregious censure of Jesus Christ—a confident and criminal leaning to human wisdom, and a robbery of the Supreme God, the Father, of his just and unalienable due." (P. 87–89.)

Again, "If Christ were not a distinct being from the Father, how could he pray to the Father?" (*Unitarian Miscell.* Vol. 1 no. 1, p. 13.)

Answer. When it is considered that Christ is also a true man as well as the Son of God in one person constituting a mediator, it is easily perceived that he sustains another relation to the Father besides his personal and filial relation. In his mediatorial character, it was meet for him to pray to his Father. He was in a state of humiliation, and needed succor of his Father; and he also offered up prayers as a high-priest for the people. That Christ in his relation to God as a mediator offered up prayers, does not overthrow his divine and filial relation. By what does Mr. Miller prove, that if Christ was one of the supposed divine persons, that in supplicating the other persons, he must have supplicated himself? It is plainly said that he prayed to his Father, not to himself. His Father is a distinct person from him. If he were not a distinct person, then indeed it might seem somewhat strange that Christ should pray to him, as the self-same person would pray to the self-same person. By what can it be proven, that it would be absurd to believe that one person in the Godhead should pray to the other: especially when such has become incarnate, and sustains the relation of a mediator? I see nothing in the Scriptures that would prove such a belief erroneous.

But if Mr. M. as well as other Unitarians presume that the above answer is not satisfactory, I shall answer according to their own theory.

Respecting the Holy Ghost Mr. M. says, "By the Holy Ghost, which the exalted Son of God received and sheds forth, I understand the Spirit of God, and not a person distinct from God. (See 1 Cor. 2:11.) 'For what man knoweth the things of a man, save the spirit of man, which is in him? Even so the things of God knoweth no man, but the Spirit of God.' Mr. Stone, in relation to this text, says, 'No one thinks that the spirit of a man means a person distinct from the man, nor can we think that the Spirit of God means a person distinct from God, for the words in the text are in the same relation.' How often do we find in the Bible the expressions, my spirit, thy spirit, his spirit, applied both to God and man? The psalmist says, my spirit faileth. The Lord says of the Son I have put my spirit upon him. If in the latter text, my spirit, means a person, distinct from the speaker so it means in the former. If so, the psalmist consisted of two persons. This none will admit." (P. 107–108. See also *Bible News*, p. 206.)

Answer. If as it is here supposed, that the Holy Spirit of God bears the same relation to God as the spirit of a man bears to man, then it irrefragably follows, that the Holy Spirit is a part of the Father's person: for the spirit of a man is the most precious part of a man's person. Thus according to Unitarians, since the Holy Ghost is not a distinct person nor being from the Father, it is plain that he is a part of the Father's person. Mr. Worcester calls him, "an *emanation* of the *Divine fullness*."

Again, Unitarians say, "We believe the Holy Ghost, or Holy Spirit, was the Spirit of God, and not a person, or being, or substance, distinct from God. When communicated to men, it was a supernatural gift, the energy and power of God operating on their minds, giving new light to their understanding, and increasing their natural intelligence and wisdom.

"That the Holy Spirit is not a person, is evident from the various characteristics attributed to it in the Scriptures. It is said to be *poured out, shed forth*, given *without measure*, and in *portions*. Men are said to *drink* into it, and it is at one time represented as being *taken away*, and at another as *quenched*. But none of these things are applicable to a person. And more especially, if the Holy Spirit were a person, and at the same time God, these characteristics would be absurd and impossible. You cannot say of God, that he is shed forth, taken away, or quenched," etc. (*Unit. Miscell.* vol. 1, no. 1, p. 17.)

If according to this statement the Holy Ghost, when communicated to men, is the energy and power of God, then by all means as he is in the Father, he must also be a divine energy and power. Energy and power essentially belong to God. The Holy Ghost, therefore, since he is not a distinct person from the Father, and yet his energy and power, it is evident that he is a part of the Father's person. According to the foregoing positions of Unitarians, it is impossible to conclude otherwise than the Holy Ghost is a part of the Father's person. For if, as they affirm, the Holy Ghost is not a distinct person from the Father, he must be a part or an appendage of the Father, or non-entity. That he is a non-entity none will admit. It is not my intention in this place to prove or say any thing with respect to the personality of the Holy Ghost; but simply to shew that Unitarians maintain positions, which if true, will inevitably prove that the Holy Ghost is a part of the Father's person.

Now since Unitarians, particularly Mr. Miller, suppose it absurd that Christ would have prayed to the Father, if he were a divine person—i. e. consubstantial to the Father—I would ask whether the Holy Ghost never prays to the Father? They will not answer contrary to the Scriptures. The Scriptures say, "Likewise the Spirit also helpeth our infirmities: for we know not what we should pray for as we ought: but the Spirit itself maketh intercession for us with groanings which cannot be uttered. And he that searcheth the hearts knoweth what is the mind of the Spirit, because he maketh intercession for the saints according to the *will* of God." Rom. 8:26, 27. "And because ye are sons, God hath sent forth the spirit of his Son into your hearts, crying, Abba, Father." Gal. 4:6. The former passage does not only prove that the Holy Ghost prays, but also that he is an intelligence: for a mind is ascribed to him.

Now, if the Holy Ghost be not a person, but that he, according to Mssrs. Miller and Stone, bears the same relation to God, as the spirit of a man bears to man, and is thus part of the Father's person, does it not follow, that when the Spirit prays, a part of the Father prays to the other part of himself? Would Unitarians call this conclusion absurd? If they do, it proceeds from their own positions. If the Holy Ghost, who according to Unitarians, if even not personally distinct, and thus something belonging to God, can pray to God, without involving an absurdity; how strange it seems, that upon the supposition that Christ is consubstantial, he could not, although, being incarnate, pray to the Father without involving an absurdity! It seems more congenial to reason that one divine person, especially when incarnate, should pray to another divine person, than that either a part, or an attribute of the self-same person, should pray to the self-same person.

Unitarians suppose, also, that if Christ were consubstantial, he could not be sent by the Father. Why not? They admit the Holy Ghost to be something pertaining to God, or to the Father's person. Is this Spirit not sent? If so, does not the Father send a part of himself?

6. Unitarians say, "Our Saviour said of himself, 'I came down from heaven, not to do *mine own will*, but the will of Him, that sent me.' (John 6:38.) 'But I have not spoken of myself; the Father which sent me, he gave me a commandment what I should say, and what I should speak.' 'As the Father *hath sent me*, even so send I you.' Let any read these passages seriously, and ask himself whether Christ, who is speaking, is the same being as the Father, who *sent* him, who taught him what he was to say, and to whose will he conformed? Would there be any meaning in these passages, if you were to suppose, that Christ alluded to himself, when he spoke of the Father who sent him?" (*Unit. Miscell.* vol. 1, no. 1, p. 14.)

Answer. It has already been proven that Christ possesses not only a human body, but also a soul, or intelligence; hence a will. Christ, although, consubstantial to the Father, hence possessing a divine and supreme will; yet also, having a human will, or a will guided by a human intelligence, it is evident that he must have an own separate will distinct from the Father's will, because the Father did not assume human nature.

The Father's will which Christ came to do was that of all

which was given him he should lose nothing, but should raise it up again at the last day. v. 39. This was effected by Christ's sufferings and death and resurrection. Christ in his sufferings manifested a two-fold volition. "And he went a little further and fell on his face, and prayed, saying, O my Father, if it be possible, let this cup pass from me: nevertheless not as I will, but as thou wilt." Matth. 26:39. Thus we see that Christ wills that the cup might pass from him; whilst, notwithstanding, he is willing that his Father's will should be done. This indicates a two-fold will. The one influenced by a human intellect, desiring to be freed from sufferings and death; the other being the same as the Father's will, would have the Father's will done, which was to effect man's salvation. This indicates a will peculiar to the Godhead, and a will peculiar to the humanity, the latter being subordinate to the former. This human will is Christ's own will, separate from the Father's will, because Christ only assumed human nature. The supposition exhibited in this objection is groundless, viz. when it is said: "Would there be any meaning in these passages, if you were to suppose that Christ alluded to himself, when he spoke of the Father who sent him?" No Trinitarian of information believes that Christ, when speaking of his Father in the aforegoing texts, alludes to himself. They believe Christ to be personally distinct from the Father; consequently, do not blend Christ's mediatorial actions with the commandments given him by his Father. They believe that as a mediator, Christ was sent and instructed by his Father, and in this respect subordinate to him. But does his subordination as a son, as a mediator, prove that his substance or divine nature is not consubstantial to the Father? By no means.

7. Unitarians proceed, p. 15: "There is another remarkable text proving the imperfection of his knowledge. When he foretold the destruction of Jerusalem, he said, 'But of that day, and that hour, knoweth no man; no, not the angels, which are in heaven, *neither the Son*, but the Father.' (Mark 13:32.) This text alone is enough to show, that the knowledge of Christ *was limited*, and that he cannot be the same as God, nor have the attributes of God."

Answer. It has already been shewn, that Christ possesses a human mind; hence a limited understanding. Christ in his humiliation according to his humanity, did not know the day and hour of the last judgment. But does it prove, that because he according to his humanity in his humiliation did not know this particular, that therefore he did not possess another nature according to which he was omniscient? By no means. As soon as it shall be proven that Christ is omniscient, it is manifest that Christ was ignorant of some things in his humiliation according to the humanity. When I shall have proven this point, it will also devolve on Unitarians to shew how Christ could have been ignorant of some things and yet be omniscient.

Unitarians admit, that all the fullness of the Godhead bodily dwells in Christ: and some also say that he is almighty by the indwelling of the Father. How is it possible for all the fullness of God to be in Christ, and yet, that he should not be omniscient? Is not omniscience belonging to the divine fullness? How is it possible that a person, who is almighty by the indwelling of the Father, should not also be omniscient? Omnipotence includes omniscience: for it is impossible for a person to be omnipotent without being omniscient.

Jesus Christ says: "and all the churches shall know that I am he which searcheth the reins and hearts: and I will give unto every one of you according to your works." Rev. 2:23. Again it is said, "But Jesus did not commit himself unto them, because he know *all men*, And needed not that any should testify of man: for he knew what was in man." John 2:24, 25. To search the reins and hearts, and to know what is in man, requires omniscience.

It cannot be denied that the Holy Ghost is omniscient. Nor will Unitarians presume to deny it. "For what man knoweth the things of a man, save the spirit of man, which is in him? Even so the things of God knoweth no man, but the Spirit of God." 1 Cor. 2:11. Since none can know the things of God but the Spirit of God, it is evident that the Holy Spirit is omniscient. Having taken it for granted that the Holy Ghost is omniscient, Christ's omniscience may be the more amply illustrated. Christ says concerning the Holy Ghost, "he shall not speak of himself; but whatsoever he shall hear, *that* shall he speak: and he will shew you things to come. He shall glorify me: for he shall receive of mine, and shall shew *it* unto you." John 16:13, 14. Now since the Holy Ghost is omniscient, and yet, does not speak of himself; but receives out of Christ's fullness that which he shews unto others, it is evident that Christ is an inexhaustible fountain of wisdom and omniscience. If it be asked, "How this omniscient Spirit could receive every thing out of Christ's fullness?," he answers the question himself: "All things that the Father hath are mine: therefore said I, that he shall take of mine, and shall shew it unto you." V. 15. Now if the Father be omniscient, possessing wisdom without measure, then surely the same is to be attributed to Christ, seeing all the Father has, is Christ's. Indeed it would be strange to suppose that the Holy Ghost is omniscient, and that he receives all things out of Christ's fullness; and yet that Christ himself is not omniscient! "In Christ are hid all the treasures of wisdom and knowledge." Col. 2:3.

Thus it is plain that Christ has a nature according to which he is omniscient notwithstanding he said in his humiliation that he did not know the day and hour of the last judgment. It must be admitted that Christ was limited in knowledge, and yet omniscient; if not, it cannot be conceived how the preceeding text speaking of his limited knowledge and omniscience could ever harmonize.

8. Unitarians urge the text in John 14:28: "My Father is greater than I," against the doctrine of Christ's Godhead. They conclude because Christ said that his Father was greater than he, that he is an inferior and a distinct being.

Answer. Christ spake of his going to the Father. "Ye have heard how I said unto you, I go away, and come *again* unto you. If ye loved me, ye would rejoice, because I said, I go unto the Father: for my Father is greater than I."

The Father was not in a state of humiliation, but was in all respects, constantly, in an uninterrupted state of glory. But Christ, although being in the form of God, yet he made himself of no reputation; he descended to the deepest state of humiliation. But by going to the Father, he would lay aside the form of a servant, and entering into the heavens, and enthroned at God's right hand he would be superlatively exalted. Christ whilst in his humiliation was less than the Father, for which reason he desired to ascend to him, that he might enjoy the same glory which he had with him before the world was. John 17:5.

Speaking after the manner of men, one man may be another's

servant, and in this relation be inferior to his lord; and yet, may possess a nature and qualities equal to his lord. If a servant were to say, "My lord is greater than I," would anyone conclude that he was also inferior to his lord with respect to his nature and qualities? By no means: for many a servant is as noble in regard to his nature and qualities as his lord. Although, the aforegoing text says that the Father is greater than Christ, yet, it does not say that the Father's nature and qualities are superior. Christ was the Father's righteous servant. Isa. 53:11. As a servant he was less than the Father, but this relative inferiority by no means proves the inferiority of his nature and qualities. One thing is to be greater in substance, but another is to be greater in a relative standing. The latter does not necessarily suppose, nor include the former.

Since Unitarians maintain that Christ's inferiority to the Father has a reference to his nature and qualities, I would ask whether this interpretation does not also oppose their own hypothesis? Although they do not believe that Christ is equal with the Father, yet they believe that he is far superior to all men and angels. But was not Christ less than angels? "But we see Jesus, who was made a little lower than the angels, for the suffering of death, etc." Heb. 2:9. Was he not obedient to Joseph and Mary? (See Luke 2:51.) Had not Pilate, and the wicked rabble of the Jews power over him? (See John 19:10, 11.) Would Unitarians admit that Christ was inferior to the angels, to his parents, and to Pilate, with respect to his nature and qualities? If they do, they cannot believe that he is the only begotten Son of God, superior to men and angels; and must thus necessarily oppose their own hypothesis. Christ even was not a man in his sufferings; the psalmist says, "I *am* a worm, and no man." Ps. 22:6.

Unitarians must necessarily admit that Christ was less than angels and men, with respect to his humiliation, but not with respect to his nature and qualities. Now if it be correct to believe, that Christ may have been less than angels and men in his humiliation without being less in nature and qualities, why may it not also be correct to believe that he could have been less than the Father in the same respect, without being inferior with respect to his nature and qualities? Whenever Unitarians shall shew a text which proves that the Father is greater than Christ with respect to his nature and qualities, then it must be conceded that Christ is not consubstantial to the Father. The aforegoing text manifestly refers to Christ's state of humiliation; hence [it] proves nothing concerning his inferiority with respect to his nature and qualities.

It is however, readily admitted, that Christ is less than the Father according to the humanity.

IMPROVEMENT

That Jesus in the fullness of time assumed a human nature and that he has once been in a state of humiliation is a doctrine sufficiently proven. But these premises Unitarians urge as objections against the doctrine of Christ's Godhead. That Christ possesses the nature and properties of a man, does not prove that he does not also possess a sublimer nature, even the nature and qualities of Jehovah. His created faculties, his human weakness in this humiliation, as little exclude from his person his uncreated, divine majesty, and glory, as the body of a man excludes from his person his intellectual faculties. Unitarians are well convinced out of the Scriptures that Christ possesses all power in heaven and in earth—in short all the fulness of Jehovah. But since they deny that he is God, they suppose that he possesses this power and glory because the Father at a certain period of time constituted him such a sublime character. Thus according to their own theory, Christ possesses the power and glory of God, though not originally; yet, by the Father's donation. They object that Christ is God, because he has limited qualities, and was subject to human weakness. But I may object in a similar manner against their hypothesis. I may say, Christ had limited qualities, he was weak; therefore it is absurd what Unitarians affirm: viz. that all power in heaven and in earth was given him; that all divine fulness dwells in him. For how can he who is limited, weak and mortal, possess all power in heaven and in earth? They would by no means admit this objection against their own hypothesis.

Whenever it shall be proven, that it is impossible for a divine person to assume a human nature, then only can this objection of Unitarians be valid. But how could this be established? There is nothing in the Scriptures, contradicting such an incarnation. All things are possible with God; therefore how strange that any one should suppose that the incarnation of the filial Godhead was impossible.

God being immutable, Unitarians suppose that Christ is not God because they conclude that in suffering and dying, he suffered a change. Some Trinitarians for the same reason suppose that a mere man suffered.

Although it has already been shewn that Christ suffered in the flesh, yet, I would ask, is it utterly incompatible with God's unchangeability for him to be grieved, or to suffer in any respect whatever?

Both Unitarians and Trinitarians admit that the Holy Ghost is God; yet in different views. The Holy Ghost, being God, is absolutely immutable. Notwithstanding, St. Paul says, "Grieve not the Holy Spirit of God, whereby ye are sealed unto the day of redemption." Eph. 4:30. To be grieved is the same as to be afflicted or to suffer. According to this, the immutable Spirit of God may be grieved, or afflicted. How he may be grieved, and yet, remain felicitous and immutable, I shall not now attempt to explain. He did not assume a human nature in his person, hence has not the medium of another nature wherein he might be grieved.

The Scriptures declare that God is more merciful than man. None will deny this, since the Scriptures abound with proofs relative to this position. But, what is mercy? It is an affection arising in the mind from the view of the misery of another, and is the result of love to that other. Or, more properly, it is a participation in another's distress or sufferings; hence is a species of suffering. (See Luke 10:33—35.)

When Ephraim was turning from his wicked ways, the Lord said, "Is Ephraim my dear son? Is he a pleasant child? For since I spake against him, I do earnestly remember him still; therefore my bowels are troubled for him; I will surely have mercy upon him, saith the Lord." Jer. 31:20. When one's bowels are troubled for another one it is an indication of a participation in suffering. That God's mercy is such a commiseration is also evident from Ps. 103:13: "Like as a father pitieth *his* children; *so* the Lord pitieth them that fear him. For he knoweth our frame; he remembereth that we *are* dust." v. 14. How does a father pity his children? A kind father when he sees his child suffer participates in the child's suffering. This no father can deny. Again, the Lord saith, "As I live, I have no pleasure in the death of the wicked, etc." (Ezek. 33, 11.) The opposite to pleasure is grief. Now, since God pities those who fear him, as a father pitieth his children, and as he has no pleasure in the death of the wicked, it is plains that he participates in the sufferings of his rational creatures. Although it may not be said that God's mercy in every particular is like the mercy of man—for it is according to his nature, and infinitely greater—yet, it must resemble the mercy of man in its leading principle: otherwise the psalmist would not have compared it to the commiseration of a human father in regard to his children. Now, such tender feelings in God, such infinite commiseration towards his creatures, do not change his nature, nor deprive him of his power, wisdom, goodness, or any of his attributes. Such as would deny these plain statements, must view God as a being who has no concern for his creatures, as an unfeeling tyrant.

Since God is merciful, and since mercy is a participation in another's sufferings, it is plain that he, notwithstanding his immutability, is susceptible of a certain species of sufferings. Now, it seems very strange indeed that all Christians admit the infinite mercy of God the Father, which, as has already been shewn, is a species of suffering; and yet, that some of them utterly deny the possibility and the fact of Christ's Godhead suffering in his humanity, which was a complete medium by which his divinity could suffer. In the same manner that some attempt to prove that Christ's Godhead could not be a partaker of sufferings: viz., in consequence of his immutability, I might also attempt to prove that the Holy Ghost cannot be grieved, and the Father cannot be merciful; since grief is the same as affliction, and to be merciful towards another, is to partake of that other's sufferings. No one can say that the mercy of God changes him; hence if such a species of sufferings is not contrary to God's immutability, Christ suffering in the flesh can by no means be derogatory to his immutability.

Since the divine nature of Christ suffered in the humanity, we see an amazing display of love which no creature can fully comprehend. Such an August person suffering could bear away the sins of the world, which would have been impossible to have been done by the sufferings of a mere creature. If the sufferings of a mere creature had been sufficient to make an atonement for sin,[*] why was it necessary that God's own Son should become incarnate? Would it not have been sufficient if some other holy person had become incarnate and suffered? Would not some of the holy angels, upon having been made flesh, have been adequate to this undertaking?

Christ partook of flesh and blood that through death he might destroy him that had the power of death; that is, the devil. Heb. 2:14. The devil is a mighty prince; hence, no mere man could conquer him. He was conquered through death; hence, there must have been a greater person in death than a mere man. Had a mere man died, how could he have raised himself up from the dead? Jesus raised himself, he is the resurrection and the life, John 11:25; therefore he was God even in death. Thus our redemption rests on a sure foundation.

SECTION V

Some arguments proving that Christ is God.

By the term *God* we understand the supreme Being. The Hebrew name *Jehovah*, signifying I AM, and which is generally rendered *Lord*, is an exclusive appellation of the supreme Being. The pious psalmist says, "That *men* may know that thou, whose name alone is JEHOVAH, *art* the most High over all the earth." Ps. 83:18. This text proves that this name is an exclusive and peculiar title of the supreme Being. By this name God called himself, when he appeared unto Moses. "God said unto Moses, I AM THAT I AM: and he said, Thus shalt thou say unto the children of Israel, I AM hath sent me unto you." Exod. 3:14. This name cannot properly be applied to any creature: for no creature can say, *I am that I am*; since every creature is subject to change every movement. I AM implies absolute immutability. Immutability is a perfection peculiar to the supreme Being.

When, therefore, it shall have been proven that this name is

---

[*] I refer the reader to my book entitled, *Answer to Mr. Joseph Moore, with a few fragments on the doctrine of justification*, in which he may see some observations on Christ's atonement for sin. See the third fragment on justification.

the proper name of Christ, then the doctrine of his eternal Godhead will also be established. Although this argument seems to be conclusive, nevertheless Unitarians suppose it to be inconclusive, since they allege that the names *God* and *Lord* are attributed to angels and magistrates. The church is called "*The Lord our righteousness.*" Jer. 23:6. Moses was also called God, "And the Lord said unto Moses, see, I have made thee a God to Pharaoh." Exod. 7:1.

To this objection I answer, that I know of no instance in the Scriptures in which an angel or a magistrate is called God in the singular number. They are called Gods in the aggregate, and figuratively, because of their offices. Neither is any angel or magistrate ever called the true or the mighty God. Moses was not called God in the unlimited sense of the word; but it is positively said that he was made a God; hence he was not God by nature, nor was he made a universal God; but only a God unto Pharaoh.

The Church being called the Lord our righteousness, is not called thus in the absolute sense of the word; but the sense in which she is so called is qualified by the addition "our righteousness"; hence *Lord* is not her proper name.

It would be absurd, to call any creature *the true God*. Jehovah (mostly rendered Lord) as a proper personal appellation is never applied to a creature. These are titles applied to the Father. They are also applied to Christ in the same sense in which they are given to the Father. With these names are connected divine attributes when applied to Christ. In all these respects the application of the titles *Gods* and *Lords* to angels and magistrates, differs totally from that of *God* and *Lord* to Christ.

Christ is called the *true God*. "And we know that the Son of God is come, and hath given us an understanding, that we may know him that is true, and we are in him that is true, *even in his Son Jesus Christ. This is the true God, and eternal life.*" 1 John 5:20. Although this text calls Christ the true God, yet Unitarians object to this assertion. They suppose that the pronominal adjective *This* does not refer to Christ, but to the Father. (See *Bible News* p. 231. James Miller vs. Isaac Lewis, p. 36, 37.) They consequently admit, if Christ was called the true God, that he would be consubstantial to the Father.

The pronominal adjective *this* cannot refer to God the Father: for the original reads thus: ουτος εστιν ο αληθινος Θεου και η ζωη αιωνιος. The translators have rendered ο αληθινος Θεου, "the true God." But it must be observed that αληθινος is an adjective in the nominative case and Θεου a substantive in the genitive case. Hence the literal translation would be "this is the true of God, and eternal life." The adjective *true* must have a substantive understood, by which the genitive Θεου is governed. The substantive understood must be *son* seeing the preceeding phrase says we are in him that is *true* or as the original reads και εσμεν εν τω αληθινω i. e. we are in the true. The next phrase shews who the one is that is *true*: viz. God's Son, Jesus Christ. The text is properly rendered thus: "And we know that the Son of God is come, and hath given us an understanding that we may know the true, and we are in the true, in his Son, Jesus Christ. This is the true (Son understood) of God and eternal life." Hence it is evident that the pronominal adjective *this* does not refer to God the Father: for it would be uncouth to say that the Father is the true Father of God. Christ being called αληηθινος, i. e. the true Son of God, it is manifest that he must be consubstantial to the Father. But the true God is understood, not a created, nor a constituted God, but a being, who is substantially and independently God. Christ being the true Son of God, hence he is not created, and as every son possesses his father's nature, even so Christ possesses the Father's substance; hence he is true God. The text does not only call Christ the true Son of God, but also calls him eternal life. Christ being eternal life, he himself must be eternal, and possess the same independent life the Father possesses. It must be remembered, that Christ does not merely like a creature, possess life, but is himself eternal life. Eternal life is the same as immortality. Immortality is an exemption from death. Eternal life is opposed to death. Immortality, or eternal life, which is the same, is a perfection and prerogative of the true God. St. Paul says, "Who (God) only hath immortality, dwelling in the light which no man can approach unto; whom no man hath seen nor can see: to whom be honor and power everlasting. Amen." 1 Tim. 6:16. If God only has immortality, then Christ is God: for his is eternal life; consequently he has immortality.

To be the true Son of God, implies to be God. Christ frequently called himself the Son of God; or, which is exactly equivalent, he called God his Father. The Jews understood this phraseology as implying that he made himself God. (See John 10, 33-38.) If the Jews had understood the term *Son of God* in a wrong sense, one should suppose that the benevolence of Christ would have required him to have rectified their error. We have no account that he ever defended himself against the accusations of the Jews, by declaring that the term *Son of God*, did not imply *to be* God. If this term denotes inferiority to the Father, why did he not defend himself against the accusations of the Jews? If Christ were not God, and if, notwithstanding, he had declared himself as such, he indeed would have been a blasphemer, and the Jews would be justifiable in having put him to death. When the Jews had accused him as a blasphemer, because he called himself the Son of God, he never denied the meaning of the term in which they understood it. That the Jews had correctly understood the meaning of this term, is evident from the evangelist's own comment. In one of these instances the *Jews* attempted to kill him for challenging this character. The words which he employed were, "My Father worketh hitherto, and I work." "*Therefore*," says the evangelist, in the following verse, "*the Jews sought the more to kill him, because he not only had broken the Sabbath, but said also, that God was his Father, making himself equal with God.*" John 5:17, 18. Thus we have the evangelist's comment on Christ's meaning in adopting this phraseology; and it is positively this: *That in declaring God to be his Father, he made himself equal with God.* If the evangelist understood the phraseology in the same sense as the Jews did, which is evident from his comment, then the proof is irrefragable, that to be the Son of God, is the same as to be God.

Christ is God according to the Father's own declaration. "But unto the Son *he saith*, Thy throne, O God, *is* for ever and ever: a scepter of righteousness is the scepter of thy kingdom. Thou hast loved righteousness, and hated iniquity; therefore God, *even* thy God, hath anointed thee with the oil of gladness above thy fellows. And, thou, Lord, in the beginning has laid the foundation of the earth; and the heavens are the works of thine hands. They shall perish; but thou remainest: and they all shall wax old as doth a garment; and as a vesture shalt thou fold them up, and they shall be changed: but thou art the same, and thy years shall not fail." Heb. 1:8–12. See Ps. 45:6, 7. Ps. 102:25–27.

When the Father in this text, calls Christ "God," ascribing to him an eternal throne; when he declares that he in the beginning has laid the foundation of the earth, and that the heavens are the works of his hands; when in declaring that the heavens shall perish, wax old and be changed, whilst he shall be the same, and his years shall not fail, he asserts his immutability, the conclusion that he is the true God, is irresistible.

In Isa. 48:12, and onward, we have these words: "Hearken unto me, O Jacob, and Israel, my called. I am He; I am the first, I also am the last. Mine hand also hath laid the foundation of the earth, and my right hand hath spanned the heavens. I call unto them: they stand up together. Come ye near unto me; hear ye this: I have not spoken in secret from the beginning; from the time that it was, there am I. And now the Lord God and his Spirit hath sent me. Thus saith the Lord, thy redeemer, the Holy One of Israel: I am the Lord thy God." Here the person speaking declares that he is the First and the Last; that he has founded the earth, and spanned the heavens; that he is Jehovah God, the Redeemer, and the Holy One of Israel; and yet he says, that the Lord Jehovah and his Spirit hath sent him: or as some have translated it; "The Lord Jehovah hath sent me and his Spirit." The person sending, therefore, is Jehovah; and the person sent is also Jehovah. Jehovah, who is sent has some of the same titles ascribed to him, which are ascribed to Jesus Christ. He is called the First and the Last, the Redeemer and the Holy One. Jesus is called the First and the Last; Rev. 1:11; he is the Redeemer, and the Holy One. Jehovah, sent by Jehovah, is therefore, Christ. The Father is never sent; Christ in the New Testament also, is said to be sent. Thus this text plainly shews that Christ is Jehovah.

The angel who appeared unto Moses (Exod. 3), calls himself the God of Abraham, the God of Isaac, and the God of Jacob, v. 6, and also I AM, or Jehovah (v. 14). This God, or Jehovah, was not personally the Father: for the term angel implies one that is sent, and the Father never is sent. The word of the Hebrew, rendered "the Lord," is not, like the English word, an appellative, expressing rank, or condition; but it is the proper name Jehovah. This proper name

Jehovah is not, in the Hebrew, a genitive after the noun substantive "Angel," as the English represents is; but the words יהוה and מלאך, "Jehovah," or "I AM," and "Angel," or messenger, are two substantive nouns, in apposition; both relating to the same person; the one refers to the appropriate name of the essence; the other to a title of office. Jehovah-Angel, would therefore be the proper translation. The Jehovah-Angel, not being the Father, must be Jesus Christ. Christ is positively called an angel. "Behold, I will send my Messenger, and he shall prepare the way, before me; and the Lord, whom ye seek, shall suddenly come to his temple; even the Angel of the covenant whom ye delight in : behold he shall come, saith the Lord of hosts." Mal. 3:1. The person called Lord and the Angel of the covenant, who should come to his temple was Christ. Christ appeared in the temple. In Luke 7:27, Christ speaking of John the Baptist, says, "This is he, of whom it is written, Behold I send my Messenger before thy face, who shall prepare thy way before thee." John the Baptist was, therefore, the Messenger, who was to prepare the way; and the Lord, even the Angel of the covenant was Christ.

Christ calls himself "I AM." He said to the Jews, "Your father Abraham rejoiced to see my day: and he saw it, and was glad. Then said the Jews unto him, "Thou art not yet fifty years old, and has thou seen Abraham? Jesus said unto them, verily, verily, I say unto you, Before Abraham was I AM." John 8:56–58. Thus according to this, Christ is the I AM, or Jehovah.

In Isa. 42:8, God says, "*I am* Jehovah, that is my name, and my glory will I not give to another." The name Jehovah implies divine perfections. It has been shewn in a former section, that the divine perfections are God's glory. Hence, since Christ is called Jehovah, he cannot be another distinct being from the Father. For if he were, another being would have God's glory, which supposition would be repugnant to the Scriptures. Therefore, Christ and the Father are consubstantial.

Christ is called the Mighty God. Isa. 9:6, "For unto us a child is born; unto us a son is given: and the government shall be upon his shoulders: and his name shall be called Wonderful, Counsellor, the Mighty God, the Father of the everlasting age, the Prince of peace." This child, this son, is the Mighty God; the Father of the everlasting age, and the Prince of peace. He who admits, that a child, a son, is the mighty God, will certainly admit, that this can be no other than Christ.

Jesus is the God of Israel. Exod. 24:9, 10, "Then went up Moses and Aaron, Nadab and Abihu, and seventy of the elders of Israel. And they saw the God of Israel. Ps. 68:17, 18, "the chariots of God *are* twenty thousand, *even* thousands of angels: the Lord *is* among them, *as in* Sinai, in the holy *place*. Thou hast ascended on high, thou hast led captivity captive: thou hast received gifts for men; yea for the rebellious also, that the Lord God might dwell *among them.*" St. Paul (Eph. 4:8) says, "Wherefore he saith, when he ascended on high, he led captivity captive, and gave gifts unto men. Now that he ascended, what is it, but that he descended first into the lower parts of the earth? He that descended is the same, also, that ascended up far above all heavens, that he might fill all things," etc. Here the apostle declares, that the person who ascended on high, and led captivity captive is Jesus Christ; and the psalmist, that the person, who ascended on high, and led captivity captive, is the Lord, who appeared in Sinai; and Moses, that the Lord who appeared in Sinai, was the God of Israel. We also know, that no man hath seen God the Father at any time. Christ is the image of the invisible God. Col. 1:15. The God of Israel was seen before and after his incarnation. This God of Israel, is Christ.

Isa. 6:1. "In the year that king Uzziah died, I saw Jehovah sitting upon a throne, high and lifted up, and his train filled the temple. Above it stood the seraphims: each one had six wings; with twain he covered his face, and with twain he covered his feet, and with twain he did fly: and one cried unto another, and said, Holy, holy, holy *is* the Lord of hosts: the whole earth is full of his glory:" and again, in the 5th, 8th, 11th, and 12th verses of the same chapter. St. John, quoting the 9th and 10th verses of this chapter, in his gospel (12:40) says, "These things said Esaias, when he saw his, *that is,* Christ's glory, and spake of him." The glory which Isaiah saw was the glory of Jehovah; yet, St. John says, he saw Christ's glory; hence Christ is Jehovah.

Christ was and shall be divinely worshipped. Divine worship is alone to be rendered to the supreme Being. This is the doctrine of Christ himself: "Thou shalt worship the Lord thy God, and him only shalt thou serve." Matth. 4:10. If it be shewn that Christ was worshipped, and that this honor is due to him, then it will also appear that he is true God.

Lest any one should suppose that the worship ascribed to Christ, implies nothing more than habitual reverence, or service, or a general course of inferior worship, it must be observed, that no only men, but also angels are commanded to worship Christ. In Ps. 97:7, "Confounded be all they that serve graven images. Worship him, all ye Gods." The person to be worshipped by all the Gods, or angels, is Christ. This is evident from St. Paul's quotation of a part of this verse in the following manner: "And again, when he bringeth in the firstbegotten into the world, he saith, let all the angels of God worship him." Heb. 1:6. That religious worship is here intended is certain: because the object of the worship commanded, is directly opposed in the command itself, to idols; and the worship, required, to that which is forbidden. Confounded be all that serve—i. e. religiously worship graven images—that boast themselves of idols. It is known that the heathens religiously worshipped idols; if they only had paid civic honors to them, they would not have been reproved by the Lord; seeing such is no where prohibited in the Scriptures. Now since not a civic, but a religious worship is forbidden to be rendered to idols, it is plain that the worship commanded to be rendered to Christ, is opposed to the worship rendered to idols; hence the worship to be paid to him must be religious.

This worship is commanded to both men and angels. "Wherefore God also hath highly exalted him, and given him a name, which is above every name; that at the name of Jesus every knee should bow, of things in heaven, and things in earth; and that every tongue should confess, that Jesus Christ is Lord, to the glory of God the Father." Phil. 2:9–11. According to this, all things celestial, terrestrial and subterranean are required to bow the knee to Christ and to confess him Lord, or Jehovah. The phrase *to bow the knee*, denotes religious worship. "I have left to me," says God to Elijah, "seven thousand in Israel, all the knees that have not bowed unto Baal, and every mouth which hath not kissed him." 1 Kings 19:18. (See Hosea 12:2.) St. Paul says, "I bow my knees to the Father of our Lord Jesus Christ." Eph. 3:14. These texts plainly prove, that *bowing the knee* implies a religious worship. To Christ, all knees shall bow and all tongues confess him Jehovah; hence all shall worship him as God. (Comp. Isa. 45:22, 23.)

We find that Christ was worshipped in great numbers of instances. In Isa. 6, the seraphim worshipped him, saying, Holy, holy, holy, is the Lord of hosts.

St. Stephen prayed to Christ. "And they stoned Stephen, calling upon *God*, and saying, Lord Jesus, receive my spirit. And he kneeled down, and cried with a loud voice, Lord, lay not this sin to their charge. And when he had said this, he fell asleep. Acts 7:59, 60. It can by no means be supposed that he should have prayed to Christ in consequence of any erroneous views: for he at that time was full of the Holy Ghost (v. 55), and therefore perfectly secured from error. No higher act of worship was ever rendered than this: seeing that he petitioned that Christ should receive his spirit, and that he should forgive the sins of his enemies. To receive one's spirit at the hour of death, implies nothing less than to grant eternal life and happiness. To do this, and to forgive sins belongs to God only. Christ is petitioned to do this by a person inspired by the Holy Ghost, therefore he is true God.

St. Paul prayed to Christ. Particularly 1 Thes. 3:11, 12:"Now God himself, and our Father, and our Lord Jesus Christ, direct our way unto you. And the Lord make you to increase, and abound, in love one to another, and toward all men, even as we do toward you." Here a prayer is offered up by St. Paul, that his way may be guided to the Thessalonians; and that they may be made to increase and abound in holiness. It is offered up to God the Father, and also to our Lord Jesus Christ, in the same manner: both being unitedly addressed in the same petition, without the least intimation of distinction.

It was the general custom among the primitive Christians to pray to Christ. They were therefore distinguished by the appellation: *"Those who called on the name of Christ."* Thus Ananias says to Christ (Acts 9:14), "Here he hath authority from the chief priests to bind all those that call on thy name." The people of *Damascus*, also, when they hear *Paul* preach, *were amazed, and said, Is not this he, who destroyed them that called on this name in Jerusalem?* Also (1 Cor. 1:1),"Paul, called to be an apostle of Jesus Christ, and Sosthenes the brother, unto the church of God, which is at Corinth, called to be saints, with all that in every place call upon the name of Jesus Christ our Lord."

Since Christ is to be worshipped, and since he has been worshipped by believers, by inspired persons, by the whole host of angels, who can Christ be? Must he not be true God, consubstantial to the Father, and distinguished by his filiation? For to God only, religious worship can be lawfully rendered. This we know from the mouth of Christ himself quoting Deuteronomy 10:20, in Matth. 4:10, "It is written, Thou shalt worship the Lord thy God, and him only shalt thou serve." God also in Exodus 34:14, says to the Israelites, "Thou shalt worship no other, God: for the Lord, whose name is Jealous, *is* a jealous God." Now if Christ be not God, God has commanded another to be worshipped; and persons under the immediate direction of the Holy Ghost, have worshipped another. Surely, it is out of the question to suppose that God should have commanded in his word that none but himself should be worshipped, and yet by his Spirit have directed persons to worship another. For in this case, he would contradict himself, which cannot be.

Although the Scriptures plainly teach that Christ is to be worshipped; yet, the *Unitarian Miscellany* says (vol. 1, no. 3, p. 105): "But we need not go further in explaining texts; for we have the express declaration of Christ himself, that he is not to be worshipped, although Mr. Emory asserts, that there is no passage in Scripture which forbids the rendering of worship to him. We beg him to open his Bible at the twenty-second chapter of Revelations, and read the eighth and ninth verses. We presume he will allow the person there speaking to be Christ. And what did he say when John 'fell down to worship before his feet?' He replied in the following remarkable words. '*See thou do it not*; for I am thy fellow servant and one of thy brethren the prophets, and of them which keep the sayings of this book. *Worship God.*' If here be not a command not to worship him, in what language can a command be uttered?"

Surely, the *Unitarian Miscellany* is mistaken; the person speaking to John in these words forbidding John to worship him is not Christ, but one of his angels. For this same 8th verse says, "and I John saw these things, and heard them, and when I had heard and seen, I fell down to worship before the feet of the angel which shewed me these things." And in verse 6th, "And he said unto me, These sayings *are* faithful and true: and the Lord God of the holy prophets sent his angel to shew unto his servants the things which must shortly be done." How plainly this verse states, that the angel shewed these things to John. And again (v. 16), "I Jesus have sent mine angel to testify unto you these things in the churches." John attempted to worship the angel of the Lord, and this angel is not willing to accept of this honor. How the *Unitarian Miscellany* could in the face of this glaring fact, declare that the person forbidding John to worship him was Christ is very strange!

Christ existed before the foundation of the world, before all creation. I apprehend in establishing this position, it will appear that Christ is from eternity. Christ, under the name of Wisdom, is said to have been before creation. Wisdom says, "The Lord possessed me in the beginning of his way, before his works of old. I was set up from everlasting, from the beginning, or ever the earth was. When *there were* no depths, I was brought forth; when *there were* no fountains abounding with water. Before the mountains were settled, before the hills was I brought forth: while as yet he had not made the earth, nor the fields, nor the highest part of the dust of the world. When he prepared the heavens, I *was* there: when he set a compass upon the face of the depth: when he established the clouds above: when he strengthened the fountains of the deep: when he gave to the sea his decree, that the waters should not pass his commandment: when he appointed the foundations of the earth: then I was by him, *as* one brought up *with him*: and I was daily *his* delight, rejoicing always before him; rejoicing in the habitable part of his earth; and my delights were with the sons of men." Prov. 8:22-31. St. Paul calls Christ the power and wisdom of God. 1 Cor. 1:24. It is thus evident that the wisdom, which was possessed by the Lord in the beginning of his way, that was before his works of old, etc. is Christ. This interpretation is also given and admitted by Unitarians.

Micah 5:2, "Whose goings forth have been from *old*, from *everlasting*." (Comp. Matth. 2:6. See also John ch. 1:1-3. ch. 17:5.)

Although Unitarians admit that Christ was before the creation of the world, yet their hypothesis will not permit them to acknowledge that he is from eternity: for if he be from eternity, then he would be true God. Mr. Worcester says, "Whatever existed before the world, may be said to be of old, from *everlasting.*" p. 224. It is evident that he supposes that *from old, from everlasting,* implies a certain period of time before the creation, in which Christ has been produced. For his positions will not permit the idea of Christ's eternal existence. *Arius,* and his followers in the commencement of the fourth century taught, that there was a time when the Son had a beginning, but that he was the first and noblest of all creatures, and that God by him as an instrument created the world.*

Thus the Arians believed that Christ was a created being, before the creation of the world. Whereas Unitarians, although they do not

---

* In order to decide this controversy, Constantine, the first Christian emperor, called a council in the city of Nice, in the province of Bythinia, in minor Asia. There were 318 bishops at this council. The first session thereof was opened in the month of June, A. D. 325. The fathers proved that Christ was called God's own Son in the scriptures. The Arians acknowledged that the Son was true God, the power, wisdom and image of the Father: thus they seemed to believe the same doctrine with the fathers of the council. Nevertheless, they afterwards declared that this predicate might also belong to such other creatures, of whom it is said, that they are created after God's own image. The fathers, therefore in order to cut of their subtilities used the word ομοουσιους which signifies consubstantial. They also drew up the following form of their creed:

"I believe in one God, the Father Almighty Maker of heaven and earth, and all things visible and invisible.

And in one Lord Jesus Christ, the only begotten Son of God, begotten of his Father before all worlds; God of God, Light of Light, very God of very God, begotten, not made, being of one substance with the Father, by whom all things were made; who for us men, and for our salvation, came down from heaven, and was incarnate by the Holy Ghost of the virgin Mary, and was made man, and was crucified also for us under Pontius Pilate. He suffered and was buried, and the third day he rose again, according to the scriptures, and ascended into heaven, and sitteth on the right hand of the Father; and he shall come again with glory, to judge both the quick and the dead; whose kingdom shall have no end.

And I believe in the Holy Ghost, the Lord and giver of life, who proceedeth from the Father and the Son; who with the Father and the Son together is worshipped and glorified, who spake by the prophets. And I believe in one holy Christian Apostolic church. I acknowledge one baptism for the remission of sins; and I look for the resurrection of the dead, and the life of the world to come. Amen."

This creed was subscribed by all the bishops of the council, except Eusebius of Nicomedia, Theognis of Nice, Maris of Chalcedonia, Theomas and Secundus of Lybia. Nevertheless, afterwards Eusebius, Theognis, and Maris, subscribed it also.

suppose that he is an absolute eternal person; yet, they do not suppose that he was created. Mr. Worcester says, "two ideas are naturally suggested by the title Son of God, viz. Divine Origin and Divine Dignity.

"By Divine Origin, I do not mean that the Son of God is a *created* intelligent Being; but a Being who properly *derived* his existence and his nature from God. It has not, perhaps, been common, to make any distinction between *derived existence*, and *created existence*; but in the present case the distinction appears very important. Adam was a *created* being; Seth *derived* his existence from the created nature of Adam; and therefore it is said 'Adam begat a son in his own likeness.' And as Seth derived his existence from the created nature of Adam, so, it is believed, the Only Begotten of The Father derived His existence from the self-existent nature of God. In this sense only do I mean to prove that the Son of God is a *derived intelligence*." (*Bible News*, p. 57. See also James Miller vs. Isaac Lewis p. 50.) Although Mr. W. admits that Christ is not created, yet he must suppose that there must have been a certain period of time before the creation of the world, in which Christ derived his existence: for to suppose that he has derived his existence from all eternity would prove him to be co-eternal God with the Father, which is the doctrine Unitarians labor to disprove.

It must be admitted that the term *everlasting*, or *forever*, frequently according to the phraseology of the Scriptures implies a period of time without endless duration. (As for instance see the following passages: Gen. 13:15. Ch. 43:9. Ch. 44:32. Ex. 12:14, 17:24. Ch. 21:6. Ch. 27:21. Ch. 28:43. Ch. 30:21. Ch. 31:16, 17. Ch. 32:13. Lev. 6:13, 18, 20, 22. Ch. 7:34, 36. Ch. 10:9, 15. Ch. 16:29, 31. Ch. 23:14, 21. Ch. 24:3. Ch. 25:30, 46. Numb. 10:8. Ch. 15:15. Ch. 18:8, 19. Ch. 19:10. Deut. 4:40. Ch. 15:17. Ch. 18:5. Ch. 28:46. Joshua 4:7. Ch. 14:9. 1 Sam. Ch. 2:30. Ch. 3:13. Ch. 27:12. Ch. 28:2. 1 Kings 12:7. 2 Kings 5:27. 2 Chron. 10:7. Heb. 10:12, 13.) But it is evident that *eternal* or *forever* can only be periodical after the existence of time. It can only be applied to created things in this sense, who live in time and who are limited. *Forever*, or *everlasting*, when applied to created things, must be according to their natures, which are limited and progressive. But when the same term is applied to God, its meaning must be according to his nature, which is infinite, without beginning or end; hence the term when applied to him means without beginning or end. His existence is not progressive; hence cannot be measured by time: he is said to inhabit eternity. Isa. 57:15. Since it is acknowledged by Unitarians, as well as by Trinitarians, that Christ existed before all creation, it will be necessary to inquire whether time was before all creation? Does time belong to creation? Time is the order of successive things in one uninterrupted or continued series: succession is that in which one thing ends or ceases to exist, and another begins; and continued is that between which no other succession can be interposed. There is therefore no time, where things do not succeed in a continued order. Hence where there is time, there must be a creation. As time is the order of the progression of things, it is evident that all things in time are subject to changes. Since all things are created, and as time is the order of the progression of things, it follows that time belongs to creation. Before creation, nothing existed but the Father, the Son and the Holy Ghost. Time did not exist; without time there is no progression of things; and without a progression of things there can be no changes; and when there are no changes, there must be immutability. Christ existed before the foundation of the world. To be before the creation of the world, implies to be from all eternity. Thus God's eternity is described: "Lord, thou hast been our dwelling-place in all generations. Before the mountains were brought forth, or ever thou hadst formed the earth and the world, even from everlasting to everlasting, thou *art* God." Ps. 90:1, 2. No one will deny that the Lord, who in this text is said to be before the mountains were brought forth, and before the earth and world was made, is the true, eternal God, the Father. Now, if to be before the creation of the world, implies nothing more than to have existed some supposed period of time before creation then did the Father also only exist some time before creation, and the phrase *"even from everlasting to everlasting thou art God,"* would also merely imply, that he had been God only for a certain space of time before creation. But as this text is a description of God's absolute, eternal existence before all worlds, even so the text in Prov. 8:22–31 is a similar description of Christ's eternal existence. If the eternity of the Father is signified by being prior to creation, is it not very strange, that when Christ is represented in language equally emphatical that he is before all worlds, that this language should not denote his eternal existence?

Unitarians admit that Christ is not a created, but a derived existence. If so, it may be asked: "Was Christ's existence derived from nothing, or from an existing substance?" If it be answered that he was produced out of nothing, then this is the idea of creation. (See Heb. 11:3.) To produce something out of nothing is creation. Mr. W. has stated that Christ has derived his existence from the self-existent nature of God, like Seth derived his existence from the created nature of Adam. If so, Christ must possess the Father's nature. No part of Christ in his pre-existent state having been created, but having derived his existence from the substance of the Father, it is impossible that he should possess other and different qualities from the Father's qualities. The Father is eternal, infinite, immutable, omnipotent, etc. Now let us suppose according to the views of Unitarians that Christ, according to his pre-existent nature, was finite, dependent changeful, etc.: would it not follow that he had other and different qualities from those of the Father? By all means. But I would ask, from what source did Christ derive these qualities? Unitarians dare not say from creation: for they deny that Christ is a created existence. Will they say that Christ derived these qualities from the Father's nature? If so, then it would follow that the Father himself was finite, dependent, changeful, etc. For Christ cannot derive any other qualities from the Father than such which the Father himself possesses. For who can possibly imagine, that Christ derived any qualities from the Father's nature, which the Father does not himself possess? If Christ be finite, dependent, changeful, etc. then surely he must have derived such qualities from the Father's nature, seeing Christ is not created. If so, then the conclusion must be that the Father himself must be finite, dependent, changeful, etc. This would be a positive denial of the Father's eternal Godhead. If Christ be not created, then he could not possibly derive any other qualities than such which the Father himself possesses. And if he has no other, he is eternal God, consubstantial to the Father.

It is acknowledged by Unitarians, and it has also been proven, that Christ created the world. The Father said to Christ, "Thou Lord, in the beginning hast laid the foundation of the earth:

and the heavens are the works of thine hands." Heb. 1:10. "All things were made by him; (the Word) and without him was not any thing made that was made." John 1:3. The creation of the world supposes an omnipotent Being. Creation is visibility of infinite power. He who is able to create atoms, may create worlds; and he who can create worlds has unlimited power and wisdom. St. Paul says, "for the invisible things of him from the creation of the world are clearly seen, being understood by the things that are made, *even* his eternal power and Godhead;" etc. Rom 1:20. Thus the creation of the worlds is a proof of the creator's eternal power and Godhead. It is so glaring that the most uncultivated nations apprehend it without any other revelation. Christ created the world, and even not one thing was made without him, that was made. The creation of the world, therefore, proves his eternal power and Godhead. How is it possible for Unitarians to deny his eternal power and Godhead, when they must own that he created the world, and when they as rational men know, that the works of creation are an infallible proof of an eternal Godhead?

The apostle says, "every house is builded by some man; but he that built all things is God." Heb. 3:4. This text plainly declares that he who built all things is God. Now Christ built all things, therefore he is God. Who can deny this conclusion?

Unitarians have admitted that the Holy Ghost is God. Mr. J. Miller says, "That the Holy Ghost is the Spirit of God and therefore God, I have never yet denied; yet I deny that the Holy Ghost is a distinct person from God, or that God and his Spirit are more persons or beings than one." (See his letters to Isaac Lewis, p. 20, 21.) Since according to Mr. M. the Holy Spirit is God, yet not a distinct person from the Father, it is evident that the Holy Ghost is identified with the Father's person, so that he is a part of the Father himself, the same as the spirit of a man is a part of the man himself. Now with respect to created persons, or intelligent beings, it is a known truth which must be acknowledged by all, and also that, that which is an essential, constituent part of one person, cannot be an essential constituent part of another person: for every created personal existence, is distinguished from every other person by its own essential, constituent parts, which can never be the essential, constituent parts of another person. If a divine person be not somewhat different in this respect, and if a divine being and person is the very same in every respect, then indeed, that which is an essential, constituent part of the Father's person, could not also be an essential, constituent part of Christ's person. But it is evident from the Scriptures, that the Holy Spirit is not only the Father's Spirit, but also, Christ's Spirit. Rom. 8:9: "But ye are not in the flesh, but in the Spirit, if so be that the Spirit of God dwell in you. Now if any man have not the Spirit of Christ, he is none of his." From this text it is very plain that God's Spirit and Christ's Spirit is the same. The proof may be thus arranged:

Christians are not in the flesh, provided God's Spirit be in them; but on the contrary, if a man have not the Spirit of Christ he is none of his. Now let us suppose for a moment, that God's Spirit was not also Christ's Spirit, how could the apostle have told the Romans that they were in the Spirit, if God's Spirit was in them, and yet deny them to be Christ's, if they had not Christ's Spirit? Is not the Spirit of the Father sufficient to sanctify a man? Should he be excluded from Christ for not having his Spirit, when yet he had the Father's Spirit? If the Father's Spirit be separate and distinct from Christ's, then a man may have the Father's Spirit without having Christ's Spirit. But is seems according to the declaration of this text, none would be a true Christian, unless he had Christ's Spirit; although it declares that if God's Spirit dwell in a man, he is not in the flesh, but in the Spirit: i. e. he is a true Christian. To be in the Spirit, and not to walk according to the flesh, is a true indication of a true Christian, and to have Christ's Spirit, and hence to be Christ's, implies the very same. Consequently, the Holy Ghost is Christ's Spirit, as well as the Father's Spirit. Again, v. 14, 15, "For as many as are led by the Spirit of God, they are the sons of God. For ye have not received the spirit of bondage again to fear; but ye have received the spirit of adoption, whereby we cry, Abba, Father." This text shews that the Spirit of God cries in the heart, Abba, Father, and St. Paul declares, Gal. 4:6, "And because ye are sons, God hath sent forth the Spirit of his Son into your hearts, crying, Abba, Father." Thus the Spirit that cries, "Abba, Father," in the hearts of believers is Christ's Spirit as well as the Father's Spirit.

Since I have irrefragably proven that the Holy Spirit is as

emphatically called the Spirit of Christ as the Spirit of the Father, if follows that this Spirit belongs to the Son's as well as to the Father's existence. If the Father would not be complete with respect to his existence without this Spirit, even so, the Son would not be complete without this same Spirit.

Two persons having one and the same spirit identified with their existence cannot be two distinct beings. The Son indeed is distinguished from the Father, and having all personal properties, he is a distinct person; yet, having the same Spirit that the Father has must be one substance with the Father; for it would be difficult to understand how two different persons, like human persons, having distinct substances, could each of them have the self-same spirit identified with their existence.

The Holy Spirit being Christ's Spirit, what must be the inference from the concession of the Unitarians? They admit that the Holy Ghost is God. If the Holy Ghost be God, and yet, as I have proven, also, the Spirit of Christ, does it not undeniably follow that Christ is God? If Christ's own Spirit be God, must he not be God himself? This Spirit belongs to Christ's existence; therefore, Christ must be God. Now Unitarians, by denying that Christ is God, must also either deny that the Holy Ghost is God, or that this Spirit is Christ's Spirit; or else they must acknowledge that Christ is true God: for it would be absurd to suppose that this Spirit belongs to Christ's existence; and yet, that Christ should not be what is a part of his own existence. Unitarians have already admitted that the Holy Ghost is God. Whether they acknowledge that this Spirit is Christ's Spirit, I do not recollect of having seen in any of their writings. Yet I presume they will not deny this, because it is proven by texts of Scripture.

Now, unless they can suppose that Christ can have a Spirit that is God, and yet not be God, they must confess that Christ is consubstantial to the Father.

There are sundry other proofs which might be alledged out of the Scriptures in support of the doctrine of Christ's Godhead, but the preceding are deemed sufficient.

SECTION VI.

The incarnation of the Son of God.

The Son of God, true God, by whom the universe was brought into existence, in the fullness of time became incarnate. In the discussion of this subject, I shall lay down the following text for my premises: "And the Word was made flesh, and dwelt among us, (and we beheld his glory, the glory as of the only begotten of the Father,) full of grace and truth." John 1:14.

The Word that was made flesh, was in the beginning with God, and was God. V. 1, 2. This shews that the Word was God; and yet, distinguished from God, for it was with God. If here two divine persons be not indicated, the phraseology must be utterly unintelligible. He who is God, certainly is a divine person; and if God be with God, the God with whom he is must be another divine person: for it would be uncouth to say that the self-same person is with himself.

The Word was in the beginning with God. I do not presume that the beginning implies God's eternity, but the commencement of creation; hence the Word already existed before creation.

This Word is a divine person, hence not a mere attribute or quality; for he is described as a person. He made the world—"all things were made by him; and without him was not any thing made that was made" (v. 3.); "he was in the world, and the world was made by him, and the world knew him not; he came into his own, and his own received him not; but as many as received him, to them gave he power to become the sons of God, *even* to them that believe on his name." v. 10, 11, 12. This is a true description of personal actions, which being ascribed to the Word, proves that the Word is a person.

It is manifest that the Word is the Son: for the text says, "and we beheld his glory, the glory as of the only begotten of the Father"; i. e. the glory of the Word is as that of the only begotten of the Father. Hence the term "*Word*" in this chapter, and "*the only begotten Son of God,*" are convertible terms.

The Word was made flesh. The term *flesh* denotes Christ's human nature. A part of human nature is here taken for the whole.

That the term *flesh* denotes human nature is manifest from the following passages: Gen. 6:12. Isa. 40:6. Joel 2:8. Matth. 24:22. Luke 3:6. Acts 2:17. Rom. 3:20. 1 Cor. 1:29. What St. John calls *flesh*, St. Paul calls *man*: "There is one God and one mediator between God and men, the man Christ Jesus." 1 Tim. 2:5.

I have already shewn that the Word is a person, and such he was from eternity. But the human nature he assumed cannot be a human person. There is but one Christ. Now if the human nature were a human person, Christ would be two persons; consequently there would be two Christs. By the term *person*, I understand a complete intelligence which is neither a part nor an appendage of another person. A man is a person; because he is a complete subsistence for himself, without being a part or an appendage of another person or existence. Thus humanity of Jesus is truly a complete human nature without sin, but is by no means a human person. Why so? Ans. The humanity of Christ was never produced to exist for itself like another man, but it was formed to be the flesh and blood of the Son of God. The humanity of Christ has, therefore, no personal existence of itself, but its personal existence is solely in the person of the Son of God.

The Word was made flesh. The Word was not made flesh, merely by dwelling in and governing the humanity. For if so, the Father would also have been made flesh: seeing the Father dwells in Christ. But no one can prove the Father's incarnation. Again, it is said, "that God dwells and walks in believers." 2 Cor. 6:16. Now, if to dwell in one would imply to be made flesh, then it would follow that God was made flesh in every saint. But this would be absurd. If to be made flesh signifies merely to dwell in the flesh, then the order of the words ought to be reversed thus: "the flesh was made the Word's, viz. the Word's dwelling."

Some deny that the divine nature was made flesh; they presume that only the person of the Son was made flesh. But if so, how could the Son be God? If the Son be God, how could the person of the Son be made flesh without God being made flesh? To say, that the Son, or his person, which is the same, but not his divine nature, was made flesh, is a positive denial of Christ's Godhead. It is very strange indeed, that any Trinitarian should deny that the divine nature was made flesh! The divine nature exists in the Son's, as well as in the Father's person. How could the Son be God, if his person was not the divine substance? Each divine person must undoubtedly be the divine substance, but in a different relation. I have already repeatedly shewn that the Father is an uncreated light and that the Son is this light reflected. Although the light reflected is distinguished from the light by which it is reflected; yet, the light reflected is substantially the same nature with the light by which it is reflected. Thus the same light exists differently, viz. not reflected, and reflected. Christ is the uncreated light reflected. Or, Christ is the divine nature reflected. Now, truly the divine nature was made flesh, but not as it exists in the Father's person, or the light not reflected; but the divine nature as it exists in Christ's person, or the light reflected was made flesh.

Such as deny that the humanity of Christ in union with the divine nature, has omnipotent power and is omnipresent, must also deny that the divine nature was made flesh, and feign that the Son's person could have been made flesh, exclusive of the divine nature: for they know if it be admitted and proven that the divine nature was made flesh, that the flesh would have omnipotent power by the divinity.

The eternal Word is God; he is therefore unchangeable. Hence when the Word was made flesh, he did not undergo a change so as either to become more perfect, or imperfect. Neither did the flesh change into the divine nature: for if so, the flesh would have lost its existence in the incarnation. But this is contrary to fact: for Christ had real flesh and blood after his incarnation.

Neither are we to suppose that the Word was made flesh, so that the Word might uphold the flesh in existence. If to be made flesh, implies nothing more than that the Word is in so far united with the flesh; so as to govern and uphold it, then it might be said, that God was personally united to every thing in existence: for he "upholds all things by the word of his power." Heb. 1:3. But this would be very absurd. Hence the personal union of the Word with the flesh cannot consist in this: that the Word merely governs and supports the flesh.

The personal union of the Word with the flesh cannot be precisely like the union between the body and the soul. The body by its members adds something to the soul, and the soul gives animation to the body. Both body and soul when united are not the same in every respect as when both are separate. The body without the soul is dead, and the soul without the body is without corporeal members. But the eternal Word is unchangeable, and is therefore, the very same after as before the incarnation and has not lost its personal unity. The Word is unchangeable and the flesh changeable, thus an unchangeable person and a changeable nature are one. Now since the Word could not have lost its personal unity by being made flesh, it is manifest that the flesh must have entered into the indivisible unity of the Word so as to have its personal subsistence in the Word, or the person of the Word has become the person of the flesh; seeing the flesh has no personal subsistence in itself. If the flesh did not enter into the personal unity of the Word, there could have been no incarnation. The Word was made flesh; the Word is a divine person, the flesh in its own nature is not a person; therefore the person of the Word has become the person of the flesh. If the Word be not the person of the flesh, how could the Word have been made flesh? The humanity did not take upon itself a divine person, nor did the divine nature take upon itself a human person, but only a human nature, which has its personal subsistence in the person of the Word.

When two created things unite together, the one cannot properly be said to have been made the other, because the union intermixes or changes their nature or properties, as, for instance, water and wine being joined together: neither the water was made wine, nor was the wine made water. For the substances are mixed, neither the water, nor the wine in this coalescence retains its own nature entire. Again, the soul and body being united, they both are not what they would be if each of them existed separately: for the soul could not operate by corporeal members, and the body would be dead. In neither of these cases is the one made the other. The water was not made wine, nor was the soul made the body: for if otherwise, the water would have all the properties of the wine, and the body the properties of the soul, and would be intelligent.

The Word was made flesh. The Word is God, hence immutable; he could therefore, in union with the flesh, neither have lost nor changed any of his properties, nor have been made more noble. But the flesh being changeful in its own nature must have entered into the unity of the Word, and thereby have obtained infinitely more than what is peculiar to its own nature, and consequently have been exalted to the summit of uncreated divine glory. For how could the flesh have entered into the unity of the Word, without being exalted, having divine glory? If the flesh entered into the unity of the Word, it must have the Word's own personal existence: for it has no personal existence in its own nature. For if Christ be also a human person, then would he be two persons; i. e., there would be two Christs, which would be repugnant to the Scriptures, seeing he is a divine person prior to his incarnation. Now if the humanity had not the personal existence of the Word for its personal existence, then would the humanity have no personal existence at all. It cannot exist like another man by itself, in its own person, but solely exists in the person of the Word. But if the humanity have the personal existence of the Word for its personal existence, then by all means the flesh must have all what its own person possesses. The flesh being no human person (but nature only) but having the Word for its person, it would appear very strange indeed that the flesh should not possess all things, all divine majesty and glory its own person possesses. Or, it would be strange, that, that which is positively belonging to the person, should not possess what the person possesses. Now let us suppose that the flesh had not thus been exalted: how could a personal union ever have taken place? For since the Word is immutable, it could receive no alteration, and if the flesh received no divine perfections, then it remained altogether in its natural state, and acquired nothing.

The sacramental controversy between Luther and Zuinglius [Zwingli], necessarily involved the doctrine of the personal union of Christ's two natures. Luther, who maintained the omnipresence of Christ's body, hence the presence of his body and blood and in the Lord's supper, believed that the person of the Word was made the person of the flesh; so that the humanity in this union, without confusion or a change of natures, is in possession of all divine attributes, and is therefore omnipotent, omnipresent, and an object of adoration. Upon this ground, as well as upon the words of the institution, he maintained the presence of Christ's body and blood in the sacrament.

Whereas Zuinglius, who denied the presence of the Lord's body and blood in the sacrament, supposed that the humanity was not susceptible of receiving such divine dignity and glory, and that it is unreasonable to believe the omnipresence of Christ's body. Calvin also (and his followers) maintained the same position.

This is one of the principal points on which the Lutheran and Calvinistic churches have been divided since the time of the Reformation. Lutherans, according to their position, suppose that the humanity of Christ in union with the Word is an object of religious worship. But Calvinists and the German Reformed must necessarily according to their principles, deny such worship to the Lord's humanity, and consider it idolatry. If Lutherans should err in this point, they must certainly be idolators; but if Calvinists err, they are in open opposition to Christ's glory in his mediatorial character, and deny him that honor which God requires men and angels to render unto him. Again, if the position of Calvinists should be correct, one of the strongest objections of Unitarians against the doctrine of Christ's Godhead will remain utterly unanswerable.

This objection shall hereafter be stated and investigated.

For the better information of the reader, I shall make a few extracts from Calvin and some of his followers, and also from Luther. Whereupon, I shall more minutely investigate the subject.

Calvin says, "Tametsi philosophice loquendo, supra coelos locus non est, quia tamen corpus Christi, ut fert humani corporis natura & modus, finitum est, Et coelo, ut loco, continetur, necesse est a nobis tanto locorum intervallo distare, quantum coelum abest a terra."

Which I translate thus: "Although, in speaking philosophically, above the heavens there is no place, nevertheless, because the body of Christ is finite as the nature and manner of a human body shews, and contained in heaven as in a place, it is necessarily distant from us by so great an interval of places as heaven is distant from the earth."

Beza, a principal Calvinistic writer, says: "Hanc enunciationem qua DEUS dicitur passus, sic interpretamur, DEUS, id est, Caro Deitati, unita est passa. Homo est omnipotens, id est, Deitas humanitati unita est omnipotens."

Which I translate thus: "In this proposition, in which God is said to have suffered we, interpret thus: God, that is the flesh united to the Godhead, suffered. The man is almighty; that is, the Godhead united to the humanity is almighty."

Again he says, "concludimus ergo, Christum non modo nolle, verum etiam NON POSSE VELLE, corpus illud suum verum & ωεριγθαπτου multis simul in locis sistere."

Translated thus: "We therefore conclude that Christ is not only unwilling, but yea, he is not able to be willing, to set up that his true and circumscribed body in many places at the same time."

Peter Martyr, another Calvinistic writer, says: "Querimur, vos dicere, Corpus Christi esse in multis locis, quodque DEI potentiam objiciatis, cum hoc ex illorum sit genera, AD QUAE DEI POTENTIA SE NON EXTENDIT."

Translated thus: "We lament that you say that the body of Christ is in many places, and that ye interpose the power of God, when this may be among the kind of those things to which the power of God does not extend itself."

Palatine Kednadon another Calvinistic writer, says: "Negamus, quod *omnipotente Dei virtute fieri possit*, ut unum & idem Christi corpus in uno loco sit circumscriptum, definitum, visibile, palpabile, alibi autem incircumscriptum, indefinitum, invisibile, impalbabile."

Translated thus: "We deny that through the omnipotent power of God it can come to pass that the one and same body of Christ is circumscribed, visible, and comprehensible in one circumscribed place, but elsewhere, uncircumscribed, unlimited, invisible and incomprehensible."

(These quotations are taken from Lucas Osiander's work.)

The following is copied from the Heidelberg catechism:

"47ste Frag. Ist dann Christus nicht bei uns bis ans Ende der Welt, wie er uns verheissen hat?

"Antwort. Christus ist wahrer Mensch und wahrer Gott. Nach seiner menschlichen Natur ist er jetzunder nich auf Erden: Aber nach seiner Gottheit, Majestaet, Gnad und Geist weicht er nimmer von uns.

"48ste Frag. Werden aber mit der Weise die zwo Naturen in Christo nicht voneinander getrennt, so die Menschheit nicht ueberall ist, da die Gottheit ist?

"Antwort. Mit nichten: dann weil die Gottheit unbegreiflich

und allenthalben gegenwaertig ist, so muss folgen, dass sie wohl ausserhalb ihrer angenommenen Menschheit, und dannoch nichts destoweniger auch in derselben ist und persoenlich mit ihr vereiniget bleibt."

Translation.

"Quest. 47th. Is not Christ then with us, even to the end of the world, as he hath promised?

"Ans. Christ is very man and very God: With respect to his human nature, he is no more on earth, but with respect to his Godhead, Majesty, Grace and Spirit, he is at no time absent from us.

"Quest. 48th. But if the human nature is not present wherever his Godhead is, are not then these two natures in Christ separated from one another?

Ans. Not at all, for since the Godhead is incomprehensible and omnipresent, it must necessarily follow that the same is not limited with the human nature He assumed, and yet remains personally united to it." (*This translation is taken from an edition printed in Philadelphia, A. D. 1812.*)

Contrary to the Calvinists and the Heidelberg catechism, Dr. Luther writes: "Cum Christus talis homo sit, qui praeter naturae ordinem cum Deo una est persona: et extra hunc hominem nullus Deus reperiatur necessario conficitur, quod etiam juxta tertium supernaturalem illum modum sit, et esse possit, *ubique, ubi Deus est*: ita ut omnia plena sint Christi, *etiam juxta humanitatem*, non quidem secundum primam illam corporealem et comprehensibilem rationem, sed juxta supernaturalem divinum illum modum.

"In hoc enim negotio fateri te oportet et dicere: Christus, secumdum divinitatem, ubi est, ibi est naturalis divina persona: et revera ibi naturaliter et personaliter est: quod perspicue ipsius incarnatio, in utero materno, testatur. Si enim filius Dei erat, certe eum personaliter esse in utero matris, et ibidem incarnari oportebat. Quod si naturaliter et personaliter est, ubi est, profecto ibidem etiam necessario homo erit. Non enim in Christo sunt duae separatae personae, sed unica tantum est persona. Ubicunque ea est, ibi est unica tantum et indivisa persona. Et ubicunque recte dixeris: hic est Deus; ibi fateri oportet, et dicere: ergo etiam Christus *Homo* adest. Et si locum aliquem monstrares, in quo solus *Deus*, non autem homo esset, jam statim persona divideretur. Possem enim tum recte dicere: hic est

Deus elle, qui non est homo, et qui adhuc, nunquam homo factus est.

"Absit autem, ut ego talem Deum agnoscam aut colam. Ex his enim consequeretur quod locus et spatium possent duas naturas separare, et personam Christi dividere: quam tamen, neque mors neque omnes Diaboli dividere aut separare potuere. Et quanti tandem, obsecro, pretii esset talis Christus, qui unico tantum loco simul divina et humana persona esset: in omnibus vero locis, duntaxat et quidem separatus Deus, aut divina persona esset, sine assumta sua humanitate. Nequaquam vero id tibi, quisquis es, concessero: quin potius quocunque locorum Deum collocaveris: eo etiam humanitatem Christi una collocare te opportebit: non enim duae in Christo naturae separari aut dividi possunt; una in Christo facta est persona: et filius Dei assumtam humanitatem a se non segregat."

"In libello, de ultimis verbis Davidis, D. Lutherus paulo ante mortem suam in hanc sententiam scripsit:"Secundum alteram temporalem humanam nativitatem etiam data est illi aeterna Dei potestas: sed in tempore, et non ab aeterno. Humanitas enim Christi non fuit ab aeterno, ut divinitas: se Jesus Mariae filius, juxta supputationem veram, hoc anno natus est annos mille, quingentos, quadraginta tres. Interim tamen ab eo momento, in quo divinitas cum humanitate unita est in unam personam, homo ille, qui est filius Mariae, revera est et vocatur omnipotens aeternus Deus, qui aeternam habet potestatem: qui omnia creavit et conservat (per communicationem Idiomatum:) propterea quod cum divinitate una sit persona, et verus sit Deus. De ea re loquitur cum inquit: omnia mihi tradita sunt a Patre. Et alibi: Mihi data est omnis potestas in coelo et in terra. Quis est ille, qui dicit MIHI? Mihi videlicet, Jesu Nazareno, Mariae filio, nato homini. Ab aeterno quidem habebam eam a Patre, priusquam homo fierem. Cum autem humanam naturam assumerem, accepi eam in tempore, secundum humanitatem: occultari autem eam, donec a mortem resurgerem, et ad coelos ascenderem: tum ea debebat manifestari et declarari, sicut Paulus dicit, eum declaratum seu demonstratum filium Dei com potentia: Johannes vocat, clarificatum, seu glorificatum." (*Concordia*, p. 784, 785.)

Which I translate thus: "Since Christ is such a man who above the order of nature is one person with God, and beside this man no God is found, it necessarily follows that he also according to the third supernatural manner is, and may be, everywhere, wherever God is; so that all things may be full of Christ, yea according to the humanity; however not according to the first corporeal and comprehensible manner, but according to that supernatural, divine manner.

"For in this matter it behooves thee to confess, and say: wheresoever Christ is according to the divinity, there he is a natural divine person, and there he is indeed naturally and personally, which his incarnation in the maternal womb plainly testifies. For if he was the Son of God, it was certainly meet for him to be personally in his mother's womb, and there become incarnate. Now since he is naturally and personally, wherever he is, he must there also be truly a man. For in Christ there are not two separate persons, but there is only one person. Wherever that is, there is the only one, and undivided, person. And whensoever thou couldst have spoken rightly: 'here is God,' then it is proper to confess and say: 'consequently, there is also the man Christ present.' And if thou canst shew any place in which God only might be, but not the man, immediately, straightway the person is divided. For then I might rightly say, here is that God, who is not man, and never heretofore was made man.

"But, God forbid that I should acknowledge or adore such a God. For from hence it would follow that place and space could separate the two natures and divide the person of Christ, which, however, neither death nor all the devils have been able to divide or separate. And finally, I ask, of how much worth might such a Christ be, who could be in one place only at the same time a divine and human person, but in all (*other*) places he would only be God, and also separated, or a person without his assumed humanity? But whosoever thou art, I shall by no means grant that to thee: but rather in whatsoever of the places thou dost place God, thou must also at the same time place the humanity of Christ: for in Christ the two natures cannot be separated or divided; in Christ the person is made one, and the Son of God does not separate from himself the assumed humanity.

"In a little book concerning the last words of David, Dr. Luther shortly before his death had written this sentence. According to the other temporal human birth, the eternal power of God has also been given to him, but in time, and not from eternity. For the humanity of Christ has not been from eternity like the divinity: but

Jesus the Son of Mary according to the true calculation is in this year, 1543 years of age. However, in the meanwhile, from the moment in which the divinity was united in one person with the humanity, that man who is the Son of Mary is indeed, and is called, the eternal omnipotent God, who hath eternal power, who hath created and preserves all things (by an idiomatical communication) therefore on that account he may be one person with the divinity and be true God. Concerning this subject it is said, when he says, 'all things are given to me by the Father'; and elsewhere, 'all power is given unto me in heaven and in earth.' Who is he, that says to me? To me, viz. to Jesus the Nazarene, born a man. I indeed had it from eternity from the Father, before I could be made man. But when I assumed human nature, I have received it in time according to the humanity, but I have kept it concealed until I rose from the dead, and ascended to heaven, then this should be manifested and declared, as St. Paul saith he was declared or manifested the Son of God with power: John calls it glorified." [*Concordia*, p. 784, 785]

According to the position of the Calvinists and the Heidelberg catechism, the divine person of God's Son is not personally united to the flesh; although the contrary is pretended. All the union admitted by them is similar to a diamond in a ring, or a planet in its orbit. This comparison has been made by some. The diamond being truly united to the ring, is still not where every part of the ring may be; and the planet being in its orbit is yet not wherever the orbit extends. Similar to this it is supposed that the divine nature of Christ is extended over the universe, and the humanity united to it, as it were at one part of the divinity in a local situation. So that the divinity might be omnipresent, and the humanity united to it, and yet be located. But it must be observed, that this, or any similar comparison, is foreign to the purpose: for the diamond is not made the ring, nor is the planet made the orbit: for if the diamond had been made the ring, and the planet the orbit, then would the diamond and the planet be wherever the ring and the orbit might be. But the Word was made flesh.

If Christ's divine nature were omnipresent without the humanity, and yet be personally united to the same, then it would follow that every saint was personally united to God: for God is united with, and dwells in, all believers; they indeed are located, whilst God united to them, is omnipresent. But can this be called a personal union? Can it be said that God was made flesh in them? By no means. The Father and the Holy Ghost also are united to the humanity of Christ. This is so manifest, that no one would attempt to deny it. But is the Father or the Holy Ghost personally united to the humanity of Jesus? Or was the Father or the Holy Ghost made flesh? By no means. Now, since neither the Father nor the Holy Ghost was made flesh, but the Son only, it must follow that the person of the Son is deeply united to the flesh, so that the flesh is wherever the Godhead may be. Thus it must be evident that the filial Godhead is more closely united to his flesh than the Father or the Holy Ghost, and therefore, exists no where without his assumed humanity.

Calvinists admit that the Son is personally united to his flesh, and yet deny that the flesh in this unity is wherever this divine person exists. They admit that Christ is a divine person who is omnipresent. Now it may be asked: is not the divine nature of Christ a person in all places, wherever he exists? Or is he a person only at one particular place? To suppose that Christ's divinity is a person at one place only would be denying his omnipresence. His person is himself; hence if his person be not omnipresent, then he himself is not omnipresent. But as it is admitted that he is omnipresent, it is also admitted that he is a person everywhere. Now if the flesh be personally united to God's Son, does it not follow that the flesh must be with this person? How can this be otherwise? The person of God's Son is omnipresent, and to this person the flesh is personally united. If the flesh be not wherever this divine person is, how can it be personally united to the same? For it would be very strange indeed to suppose that the flesh is personally united to the Son of God, and yet not to exist where the Son of God exists.[*]

Christ, in so far as he is the second Adam, i. e., in so far as he is man, having been made a quickening Spirit, proves a communication of divine attributes by virtue of the personal union with the Word. The flesh of Jesus has become full of immortality. He says, "I am the

---

[*] The reader will please observe that the author had written several more arguments on this subject, which were to succeed these; but they were lost in transmitting per mail; & before the author could refurnish them he was called off by an untimely death.

living bread which came down from heaven: if any man eat of this bread, he shall live forever: and the bread that I will give is my flesh, which I will give for the life of the world." John 6:51. And v. 54–56, "Whoso eateth my flesh and drinketh my blood hath eternal life, and I will raise him up at the last day. For my flesh is meat indeed, and my blood is drink indeed. He that eateth my flesh, and drinketh my blood, dwelleth in me, and I in him."

Now since Christ's flesh is the living bread that came down from heaven, and can cause eternal life in those who partake of it, the conclusion is that it must have such source of life by the Word with whom it is personally united: for the flesh without this union, in its own nature, could not possess immortality: because to have immortality is God's prerogative. By the personal union with the Word, the flesh without all contradiction possesses an inexhaustible fountain of life and miraculous gifts. By touching his sacred flesh, healing gifts issued to cure diseases: as for instance when the woman that was diseased with an issue of blood, had touched his garment was made whole. Matt. 9:20–22. Again, "And the whole multitude sought to touch him; for there went virtue out of him, & healed them all." Luke 6:19. Now I would ask, could such miraculous virtues have proceeded out of Christ's flesh so as to cure the most inveterate diseases; virtues that were truly divine, if the flesh had not divine attributes? By no means. No one could touch this sacred flesh without touching the eternal Word, or filial Divinity. The divine, invisible power and glory were rendered visible and palpable through the flesh. Hence St. John says, "That which was from the beginning, which we have heard, which we have seen with our eyes, which we have looked upon, and our hands have handled, of the Word of life; &c." 1 John 1:1. Christ according to his divine nature is invisible and impalpable; hence if the apostles could see and handle this eternal Word of life, how could they do it otherwise than by seeing and handling his humanity? His humanity being filled with the fullness of the Word, the Word himself was seen and handled by the apostles in seeing and handling the humanity: for the Word was made flesh. The Word's glory became visible: for says St. John, "and we beheld his glory, the glory as of the only begotten of the Father, full of grace and truth." Ch. 1:14. as little as a coal has the virtue of itself to burn, but has it by the fire in it, even so little has the flesh of Christ in its own nature healing virtues and omnipotent power, but has such really imparted by the personal union with the Word.

It has already been shewn that the Holy Ghost is Christ's, as well as the Father's, Spirit. Although it cannot be said that the Holy Ghost was made flesh, yet as this Spirit is the Spirit of the Son, the flesh also became a partaker of this Spirit. Christ was anointed with the Holy Ghost. For this reason he is called Christ, which word signifies one that is anointed. He was not anointed according to his divinity, because the divinity always had this Spirit: the humanity therefore, must have received this holy unction. I would, however, not presume to affirm that the humanity was anointed by virtue of the Word's incarnation. It indeed would follow that the humanity would have been anointed by and through the incarnation, provided the Holy Ghost was only the Son's, and not also the Father's, Spirit. But since he is also the Father's Spirit, the humanity could not have been anointed merely in consequence of the Son's incarnation: for if the incarnation only were the cause of the anointing, then it would follow that the Father also had been made flesh, which is contrary to the Scriptures. Since the Holy Ghost is not the Son's spirit alone, but also the Father's, therefore, as the Father was not incarnate, the humanity was anointed, not by virtue of the incarnation, nor by the Son only, but by the Father also. The reason assigned why he was anointed was because he loved righteousness and hated iniquity: "Thou hast loved righteousness and hated iniquity; therefore God, even thy God, hath anointed thee with the oil of gladness above thy fellows." Heb. 1:9. Thus we sees that he was not anointed merely in consequence of his incarnation, but because he loved righteousness and hated iniquity.

It must be confessed that the personal union of the flesh with the Word is the original cause why the humanity is in the form of God, and is a partaker of infinite attributes; but when the Father anointed him with the Spirit, he then particularly received special gifts and glories as a man, by which his human intellects became enlarged, and by which he as man is ornamented with a fullness of gifts above all men and angels: "for he was made much better than the angels, as he hath by inheritance obtained a more excellent name than they." Heb. 1:4. He was anointed in his state of humiliation, i.e., before his resurrection: for at his baptism in Jordan the Spirit of God descended upon him like a dove. Matt. 3:16. After which time he began his public ministry: for then the Spirit of the Lord was upon him, because he had anointed him to preach the gospel to the poor; he had sent him to heal the brokenhearted, to preach deliverance to the captives, and recovering of sight to the blind; to set at liberty them that are bruised; to preach the acceptable year of the Lord. Luke 4:18, 19—and to perform divine miracles of benevolence. The prophets and apostles were inspired by the Holy Ghost, but they had received the Spirit by measure; but Christ was not only anointed with the oil of gladness above his fellows, but he received the spirit without measure. John 3:34.

The humanity of Christ by the personal union with the Word has divine power and glory and also was particularly anointed with the Holy Ghost without measure; he is, therefore, worthy of adoration and is the most lovely and beautiful of all objects in creation.

The humanity of Jesus was undoubtedly glorified, not with a created but an uncreated glory. Just before his crucifixion he prayed to his Father: "And now O Father, glorify thou me with thine own self, with the glory which I had with thee before the world was." John 17:5. We know that the Father always granted his prayers; hence Christ was glorified with the glory for which he prayed. Christ, being consubstantial to the Father according to his divine nature, could not have prayed to be glorified according to this nature because it is unchangeable and therefore could not have been restored to its pre-existent glory. Christ in so far as he is a mediator offered prayers to the Father; hence in this character he prayed to be glorified. This shews that Christ had a glory with the Father before the foundation of the world; this he had as eternal God by the Father; it also shews that he desired to be glorified in time as a God-man with the same glory. This pre-existent or divine glory is no created glory: for it existed before creation; hence it is the glory which is peculiar to, and the prerogative of, the Supreme Being. Now since Christ desired to be glorified in time with this glory, he must have received it according to his humanity; hence his humanity in its re-exalted state has the full exercise of all infinite attributes, or the uncreated glory of God.

Calvinists who deny that the humanity has received such glory are not able to explain this text otherwise without denying Christ's eternal Godhead. For if they say that he was glorified according to his divine nature, it will then prove that he according to this nature was for awhile destitute of this divine glory; consequently, must have changed, which supposition would be contrary to the idea of his being eternal God, who is in his own nature immutable. To suppose that this glorification did not really happen to Christ's person, and that he was only glorified in the sight of intelligent creatures, is out of the question; for the text says, "O Father, glorify thou me with thine own self"; hence not merely in the sight of intelligent creatures. Thus was Jesus glorified, though no creature should have known it.

Now since I have irrefragably proven that Christ in his mediatorial character received the uncreated glory of God, even that which he had before the foundation of the world, it is unquestionably proven that the humanity possesses infinite, divine attributes.

In speaking on the re-exaltation of Christ according to his humanity, I would not wish to be understood to say that he in his state of humiliation had utterly lost his divine glory which he had by the personal union with the Word, which he again received in the exaltation. St. Paul affirms of Christ Jesus that he was in the form of God during his state of humiliation. Phil. 2:6–8, "Who being in the form of God," i. e., in the meanwhile that he had made himself of no reputation, and had become obedient unto death. See v. 7, 8. The Greek participle υπαρχωγ is in the present tense, signifying *existing* or *being*. That is, he was existing in the form of God during his humiliation. He therefore had never laid the form of God aside, even in his deepest humiliation. For he had during his public ministry, performed many miracles which required a divine power. He says in this state, "I have greater witness than that of John: for the works which the Father hath given me to finish, the same works that I do bear witness of me, that the Father hath sent me." John 5:36. At his rebuke the winds and the sea were calm, so that the men who were with him in the ship marveled, saying, What manner of man is this, that even the winds and the sea obey him! Matth. 8:26, 27.

To suppose that Christ was in the form of God according to his Godhead, would be the same as to say that God was in the form of God, which would be uncouth. There would be no sense in affirming that God was in the form of God. Hence Christ in his mediatoreal character, or incarnate state was in the form of God. For by the incarnation a divine visible form was seen, beaming forth with divine splendour. Christ having this divine form throughout his state of humiliation, shews that he had never laid aside his divine attributes. His humiliation, therefore, consisted in acting like a servant; in being obedient unto death, even the death of the cross. In these respects he had no use of his power and glory: for if he would suffer abuse from his enemies, and lay down his life, he must become passive. Being passive in these respects was indeed a very deep humiliation.

His re-exaltation consisted in being freed from sufferings and death, and in having the full use and exercise of his divine power and glory after his resurrection. He was "declared to be the Son of God with power according to the spirit of holiness, by the resurrection from the dead." Rom. 1:4. Christ's humanity in this exalted state is not only personally united to the Word, and has a source of infinite power and glory, but he is also enthroned at the Father's right hand, exercising divine prerogatives and reigning in the plenitude of power.

The humanity of Jesus thus glorified is truly omnipresent. The Word was made flesh. The Word is God; God is omnipresent, the flesh is therefore one thing with the Word, hence omnipresent: for it is out of the question to suppose that the Word has any thing nearer to himself than his assumed humanity. Christ said, "Where two or three are gathered together in my name, there am I in the midst of them." Matth. 18:20. To be in the midst of every two or three assembled in Christ's name over the whole world, requires omnipresence. Although this text be sufficiently explicit in itself to prove Christ's omnipresence—hence the omnipresence of his human nature, seeing that pertains to his person—yet because Calvinists suppose that the idea of the omnipresence of a body is repugnant to reason and the principles of philosophy, they give this text an explanation contrary to its reading, and say, instead of Christ being in the midst of two or three assembled in his name, that his spirit only is in their midst, when yet it is evident that the person who is God-man is in their midst. The appellation *Christ*, in their views on this text, means his Godhead only, and thus they separate his humanity from his person, and make void the doctrine of the Word's incarnation.

The principal objection against the omnipresence of Christ's body is founded upon supposed reason. It is said two bodies or substances cannot at the same time fill the same space, and that if a body were everywhere present, it would fill up all space so that no other creature could exist. Again, some say, it would require an immense body in size to be every where present. Since Christ possesses a real human body of an ordinary size, it is concluded that it cannot be omnipresent.

This pretended reasoning is not reason, but a sophism. The premises of this objection are: *a mere human body or created substance has its ordinary size bounded by space*; and then the conclusion is brought in: *therefore the body of Christ cannot be omnipresent.* Calvinists believe that Christ was born a man of the virgin Mary without a human Father. This is according to truth. But I might oppose this doctrine upon a similar ground. I could say: no man is born without a human father, therefore it is contrary to reason to believe that Christ had no human father. This, though similar to the position of Calvinists, would be a sophism. Though all men descend from human fathers, yet it does not follow that the humanity of Jesus was not produced without a father because the virgin Mary conceived not in an ordinary manner, but by the energy of the Holy Ghost. Again, Calvinists admit and teach that Christ's Spirit is everywhere present; although they deny the omnipresence of his body. Now I may also object to the omnipresence of Christ's Spirit upon a similar ground. I can say no created spirit, whether an angel or the soul of a man, can be omnipresent: for no man can possibly think on two things at the very same instant; therefore Christ's Spirit cannot be omnipresent. This truly would be a sophism. For what may be affirmed of a created spirit cannot be applied to an uncreated Spirit, who is God. A created spirit is present like a creature, but an uncreated Spirit is God, and therefore is omnipresent. The body of Jesus, though created, yet does not sustain the same relation of other bodies, nor exist in the same manner. Other men's bodies are not the bodies of the Son of God; they have their subsistence in human persons; whereas the body of Christ is the body of the Son of God and subsists in his divine person: for the Word was made flesh. Now to conclude that because a mere man's body is not every where present, that therefore Christ's body cannot be omnipresent, is unfair and sophistical. If his body were the body of a mere man, the conclusion would be correct. But since his body is the body of the Son of God, it is in a far different state from all other bodies. Though a created body, having according to its own nature a limited presence, yet by the personal union with the Word, it has obtained an uncreated presence, or rather the omnipresence of God. The body of Jesus therefore is omnipresent—not after the manner of a created substance, but after the manner of God, i. e. it is omnipresent like God is omnipresent.

Do Calvinists suppose that if the body of Christ were omnipresent that it could not be omnipresent but by an extension of parts filling the universe with a created dimension? It seems that they entertain this idea: otherwise they would not object to the omnipresence of Christ's body, upon the ground that two bodies or substances cannot at the same time occupy the same space. If there can be no omnipresence without an extension of parts filling all space, how can God as God be omnipresent? Would it not also follow that God's parts would be extended over the universe like the air? If so, would he not also occupy the space of every creature, and would not then every creature be forced out of existence? Whether any of the Calvinists believe that God is omnipresent by extension of parts I do not presume to affirm. But it is out of the question to suppose that God is omnipresent by extension of parts, diffusing himself over all creation like the subtile air; for he is unchangeable. Before the world or any thing was created, God could not have been everywhere present. For it is impossible for a being to be present in a place when no place exists. Before any thing was created, nothing could have existed but God. But where did he exist? In no world, in no place, but in himself, in his uncreated glory. In short, he existed out of all creation, and could therefore not have been omnipresent by extension of parts. Since the creation he did not change; and although he operates upon, and is present with, all creatures and in all places, yet does he not extend his parts, nor is he confined by any creature, nor limited by locality. Thus it is evident that God is omnipresent, not like a created substance would be in a place, but after an uncreated manner, peculiar to his own nature. Now since the body of Christ is personally united with the Word, it has received the uncreated omnipresence of God, and is therefore not omnipresent like a creature would be present in a place; hence it is in vain to urge any objection founded upon a creature presence. Before the doctrine of the omnipresence of Christ's body ought to be pronounced unreasonable, it ought first be proven that it was impossible for the Son of God to receive the humanity into his own person, or for the Word to have been made flesh. By what can it be proven that the Word could not have received the humanity into his person? Or by what text can it be proven that it was not received into the Word's person? Is the mere assertion of men to be taken as evidence?

To say it is impossible for a being to have a limited and visible presence and yet, at the same time, to be omnipresent and in all other places to be invisible, is contrary to fact.

God as God, before the incarnation in sundry instances, manifested a visible and local presence, whilst at the same time he was omnipresent, and in all other places invisible. It is said that "Cain went out from the presence of the Lord, and dwelt in the land of Nod, on the East of Eden." Gen. 4:16. Is not the presence of the Lord everywhere? By all means: for this is clearly revealed in the Scriptures. How, then, could Cain have went out from the presence of the Lord and dwell in the land of Nod? The Lord had a limited presence: otherwise Cain could not have went out from it. It seems this presence was not in the land of Nod, because when Cain was in it, he was out of the Lord's presence. Again, when Adam and Eve, "heard the voice of the Lord God walking in the garden, in the cool of the day: they hid themselves from the presence of the Lord God amongst the trees of the garden." Gen. 3:8. The Lord walking in the garden proves that he moved; hence had occupied space, and that Adam and Eve hid themselves from his presence, shews that he had a limited, visible presence: for it would have been impossible for them to have hidden themselves from his unlimited, invisible presence.

Again, upon the prayer of Moses the Lord God caused his glory to pass by and his back parts were seen by Moses. Exod. 33:22, 23. This again proves that God had a limited, visible presence, whilst he was omnipresent, and at all other places invisible. Many more instances might be adduced from the old Testament, by which it could be made appear that God had a limited, visible presence, though an Omnipresent Being—but I deem these already mentioned sufficient. I will yet observe that a being that can be seen by finite beings, must have a limited, visible presence: for no creature could see God in all places unless the same could also be in all places. Although God may not be seen by us in the present state of mortality; yet, if we become pure in heart we shall hereafter see him. "Blessed are the pure in heart: for they shall see God." Matth. 5:8. "Beloved, now are we the sons of God, and it doth not yet appear what we shall be: but we know that, when he shall appear we shall be like him; for we shall see him as he is." 1 John 3:2. These texts most unequivocally prove that believers shall see God even as he is. Although their bodies shall be raised up from the dead and be clothes with immortality; yet they will remain finite creatures. Now if they shall see God, does it not follow that God in heaven has a limited, visible presence; whilst he is also in other respects invisible and omnipresent?

Having positively proven that the eternal God has a limited, visible presence, whilst yet he is invisible and omnipresent; how then can any man say with propriety, that it is absurd to believe that the body of Christ can be visible and limited in one place, and yet in other respects be invisible and omnipresent? It is in vain to argue [that] because Christ, when upon earth, had a limited, visible presence, and that when he ascended to heaven he has also somewhere a glorious, visible presence, that therefore his humanity (in so far as it is personally united with the Word) is not also invisible and omnipresent. For the visible and limited presence of Christ's body proves nothing against its invisible omnipresence. If it did, it would also prove that God as God, could not be invisible and omnipresent; because I have shewn that he has a limited, visible presence.

Now the following objection may easily be answered: viz. Christ ascended up to heaven, and he shall come again; now if he were already present, why then would it be necessary for him to come? Those who make this objection admit that God's Spirit is omnipresent; hence I would also ask them, why did Christ say, "If I go not away, the Comforter will not come unto you; but if I depart, I will send him unto you." John 16:7. Why was it necessary that the Comforter, i. e. the Holy Spirit, should come when he was already omnipresent? Whatever may be answered to this question, may also be answered with respect to the coming of Christ. If it be said that the coming of the Holy Ghost implies a visible manifestation of the Spirit on the day of Pentecost, I may with equal propriety affirm that the coming of Christ implies the manifestation of his visible presence from heaven to judge the world. But neither the visible manifestation of the Holy Spirit, nor of Christ, proves away the invisible omnipresence of either.

The Heidelberg Catechism, in order to prove that the humanity of Jesus is not omnipresent, marks the following passages:

Matth. 26:11: "For ye have the poor always with you; but me ye have not always." This text does not say one word that the humanity of Christ is not omnipresent. It alludes to a good work performed upon his body: For, a certain woman having poured a precious ointment on his head, his disciples had indignation when they saw it, saying, to what purpose is this waste? For this ointment might have been sold for much, and given to the poor; verse 7-9. Whereupon Jesus said unto them, Why trouble ye the woman? For she hath wrought a good work upon me. For ye have the poor always with you; but me ye have not always. V. 10, 11. Now it is manifest that they would not always have Christ in a visible manner, so that they could anoint his body. That he afterwards withdrew his visible presence, and needed nothing for the comfort of his body, does by no means prove that his body has not an invisible, divine omnipresence. There is a considerable difference between saying that his disciples should not have him any more in a visible manner, so that they might administer comforts to his body such as anointing him with precious ointment; and that he would not be omnipresent.

Heb. 8:4: "For if he were on earth, he should not be a priest." Christ's visible, limited presence, as it once was in his humiliation, is no more on earth.

It is evident from the context that Christ was exalted at God's right hand; hence is no more on earth in a state of humiliation, but is truly omnipresent: "We have such an high priest, who is set on the right hand of the throne of the Majesty in the heavens." V. 1. To sit at the right hand of God is opposed to be[ing] on earth in a state of humiliation, and positively implies to be omnipresent and to reign with omnipotent power.

John 16:28: "I leave the world and go to the Father." That Christ left the world by withdrawing his visible presence is evident from the context. But how that his leaving the world and going to the Father, should prove that his body is not omnipresent, is indeed very strange. If he went to the Father, where can he be? Is it not acknowledged by all that the Father is omnipresent? If Christ, according to his humanity, went to the Father, it is so far from proving that the same is not omnipresent, that it establishes its omnipresence. For if Christ went to the Father, then he must be wherever the Father may be, but the Father is omnipresent.

When Christ ascended to heaven, he was also exalted at God's right hand. "He is gone into heaven, and is on the right hand of God; angels and authorities and powers being made subject unto him." 1 Pet. 3:22. If it be asked, "According to which nature was Christ exalted at God's right hand?" It must be answered, according to his human nature. It has already been shewn that he humbled himself according to this nature; for he was put to death in the flesh. 1 Pet. 3:18. And as this exaltation took place in consequence of his preceeding humiliation, it is evident that the humanity was exalted. His divine nature as such is not susceptible of being thus exalted, because it is the divine majesty and glory itself.

As the Scriptures represent God as having eyes, ears, mouth, hands, etc., it follows that the right hand of God is a part of himself. When I say the hand of a man, I mean it to be one of his members, pertaining to his person. If God have hands as the Scriptures plainly shew, then his right hand is one of his members inseparable from himself. The right hand of God is therefore as little confined by space and locality and his Being. The right hand of God destroyed Israel's enemies. "Thy right hand, O Lord, is become glorious in power: thy right hand, O Lord, hath dashed in pieces the enemy." Exod. 15:6. (See Ps. 18:35. Ps. 118:15, 16.) Again, the Lord says, "Mine hand also hath laid the foundation of the earth, and my right hand hath spanned the heavens." Isa. 48:13. The hand of God having laid the foundation of the earth, and his right hand having spanned the heavens proves that his right hand is his Almighty power and infinite majesty. No angel, however dignified he may be, was ever told to sit at God's right hand: "But to which of the angels said he at any time, sit on my right hand, until I make thine enemies thy footstool!" Heb. 1:13. To be at God's right hand is the same as to possess infinite power and glory.

The right hand of God is omnipresent. "Whether shall I go from thy spirit? Or whither shall I flee from thy presence? If I ascend up into heaven, thou art there: if I make my bed in hell, behold, thou art there. If I take the wings of the morning, and dwell in the uttermost parts of the sea; even there shall thy hand lead me, and thy right hand shall hold me." Ps. 139:7-10. From these passages it is sufficiently manifest that the right hand of God is Almighty and omnipresent.

Now since the humanity of Jesus was exalted at God's right hand, it must consequently have the full exercise of Almighty power, and be every where present. This man Jesus, who is our brother, is in the heavens enthroned at God's right hand and is worshipped by angels. That nature according to which he was highly exalted, and according to which he received a name which is above every name, is to be worshipped in union with the divinity. "Wherefore God also hath highly exalted him, and given him a name which is above every name: that at the name of Jesus every knee should bow, of things in heaven, and things in earth, and things under the earth; and that every tongue should confess that Jesus Christ is Lord, to the glory of God the Father." Phil. 2:9-11. "And I beheld, and heard the voice of many angels round about the throne, and the beasts and the elders: and the number of them was ten thousand times ten thousand, and thousands of thousands, saying with a loud voice, Worthy is the lamb that was slain (*he was slain according to the flesh*) to receive power, and riches, and wisdom, and strength, and honour, and glory, and blessing." Rev. 5:11, 12.

How highly is this man Jesus dignified by heavenly hosts! O my soul, rejoice in his exaltation. He arose with the same body: for he shewed his wounds to his disciples, and ascended with it to his Father. How highly is human nature ennobled by the exaltation of Jesus! Now is it possible that vain philosophy should prevent so many who profess themselves Christians from acknowledging this glory and dignity to this man their brother, and refuse to worship him, whom all the angels in heaven worship! Let such who have hitherto denied this divine dignity and glory of the man Jesus ponder on these remarks. This man exercising universal dominion at God's right hand, proves that we need not fear death, nor the powers of hell: for he having the keys of hell and of death, has them under his control so that they cannot injure us. He being exalted as man, he can succour us in this world of temptation. As a high priest upon the throne of glory, he having himself been tempted and felt all the miseries of human life, is able and willing to direct all things for the benefit of his brethren. "Wherefore in all things it behooved him to be made like unto his brethren, that he might be a merciful and faithful high-priest in things pertaining to God, to make reconciliation for the sins of the people. For in that he himself hath suffered, being tempted, he is able to succour them that are tempted." Heb. 2:17, 18.

Although Christ having ascended into the heavens; yet he is with his Church, not only as God, but also as man: for by his exaltation he has the exercise of all power and dominion. "Now that he ascended, what is it but that he also descended first into the lower parts of the earth? He that descended is the same also that ascended up far above all heavens, that he might fill all things." Ephes. 4:9, 10. Christ ascended according to his body. This no one denies. Now if he ascended up far above all heavens, can he be confined in any one particular heaven, or contained in a place? He that is far above all heavens, is he not exalted at the summit of Jehovah's uncreated glory, and must he not be omnipresent? Can any thing be higher than the heavens, but God? The text says that he ascended far above all heavens, that he might fill all things. He that fills all things—hence the universe—must undoubtedly be omnipresent. By Christ's ascension he fills all things, which proves that by his exaltation he got the exercise of all dominion. His ascension, therefore, is so far from proving that he is not omnipresent that it establishes his omnipresence. When Christ fills all things, no place can be found where he is not present.

After Christ's glorious ascension, St. John the Divine saw him in a vision walking in the midst of the seven candlesticks, i. e., in the midst of his Church. He saw him as the Son of Man; for he describes his head, hairs, eyes, feet, right hand, etc. which are members indicating his human body, Rev. 1:13-17. Now when John saw the glorified body of his Jesus in the midst of the churches, it proves his omnipresence, and a knowledge of it proves a great consolation to all believers.

FINIS